CodeIgniter for Rapid PHP Application Development

Improve your PHP coding productivity with the free compact open-source MVC CodeIgniter framework!

David Upton

[PACKT] PUBLISHING

BIRMINGHAM - MUMBAI

CodeIgniter for Rapid PHP Application Development

**Improve your PHP coding productivity with the free compact
open-source MVC CodeIgniter framework!**

First published: July 2007

Production Reference: 1160707

Published by Packt Publishing Ltd.
32 Lincoln Road
Olton
Birmingham, B27 6PA, UK.

ISBN 978-1-847191-74-8

www.packtpub.com

Cover Image by Vinayak Chittar (vinayak.chittar@gmail.com)

Credits

Author

David Upton

Reviewers

Rick Ellis

Derek Allard

Development Editor

Douglas Peterson

Assistant Development Editor

Nikhil Bangera

Technical Editor

Ajay S

Editorial Manager

Dipali Chittar

Project Manager

Abhijeet Deobhakta

Indexer

Bhushan Pangoankar

Proofreader

Chris Smith

Production Coordinator

Shantanu Zagade

Cover Designer

Shantanu Zagade

About the Author

David Upton is a director of a specialized management consultancy company, based in London but working around the world. His clients include some of the world's largest companies. He is increasingly interested in web-enabling his work, and seeking to turn ideas into robust professional applications by the simplest and easiest route. He has so far written applications for two major companies in the UK. His other interests include simulation, on which he writes a weblog that takes up far too much of his time, and thinking.

I'd like to thank Rick Ellis for writing CI and for making it available, free. This spirit of generosity with such valuable intellectual property is what makes the Open Source movement a success, and an example to the rest of us.

I'd also like to thank Rick, and Derek Allard, for undertaking a technical review of the book and making many helpful suggestions.

Mark Barker inspired and helped me to understand Object Orientation, during many Saturday evening 'geek-outs'.

Lastly, but not least, my thanks to Julia, John, and James for their love, support, and patience.

About the Reviewers

Rick Ellis is the founder and CEO of EllisLab.com, the company that develops CodeIgniter and several other widely used web applications. Rick Ellis has a diverse background in media technology, having worked in creative and technical capacities on interactive projects for Disney, to feature films for Oliver Stone, and almost every kind of web-based project in-between.

Derek Allard is a programmer, author, and award-winning instructor based in Toronto, Canada. He builds web applications, is a standards and accessibility supporter, a scripting and database guy, and a PHP junkie. A sought-after educator and freelancer, Derek spends most of his time working with XHTML, PHP, XML and JavaScript.

As a highly visible CodeIgniter community member, Derek was hired by EllisLab as the Senior Technical Support Specialist. He devotes time to ensuring CodeIgniter and their flagship content management system, ExpressionEngine, remain market leaders.

He blogs about all things web at www.derekallard.com.

Table of Contents

Preface   **1**

Chapter 1: Introduction to CodeIgniter   **7**
  What can CodeIgniter Do for You?   **7**
    Save Time   8
    Make Your Site More Robust   9
      Keep Your Links Up-To-Date Automatically   9
      Save Database Crashes: 'prep' Your Data Entry Forms   10
    Make Your Code Bolder   11
      Send Email Attachments without Hassles   11
      Save Bandwidth by Zipping Files That Users Need to Download   12
  Yes, But...What is CodeIgniter? What are Frameworks?   **12**
  And Who is That Man?   **14**
  The 'Open Source' Business Model   **15**
  What CI Doesn't Do   **16**
  License   **18**
  Summary   **19**

Chapter 2: Two Minutes' Work: Setting up a CodeIgniter Site   **21**
  Prerequisites   **21**
  Installing CodeIgniter   **22**
  Exploring the File Structure   **23**
  The Configuration File   **24**
  Does it Work?   **25**
  Summary   **25**

Chapter 3: Navigating Your Site   **27**
  MVC—Just Another Acronym?   **28**
  The Structure of a CI Site: Controllers and Views   **29**
    The Welcome Controller   31
    Working with Views   32

The Default Controller	33
CodeIgniter Syntax Rules	**33**
Controller	34
View	34
Types of Files or Classes on a CI Site	**34**
What are All Those Folders For?	**37**
Designing a Better View	**37**
Designing a Better Controller	**39**
Getting Parameters to a Function	40
Passing Data to a View	41
How CI Classes Pass Information and Control to Each Other	**43**
Calling Views	43
Calling Functions Directly	43
Interacting with Controllers	44
It's Just Like an Egg-Cup	45
An Example of a CI Helper: the URL Helper	46
A Simple Library Example: Creating a Menu	48
Summary	**49**
Chapter 4: Using CI to Simplify Databases	**51**
Configuration Settings	**51**
Designing the Database for Our Site	**52**
Active Record	**53**
Advantages of Using the Active Record Class	54
Saving Time	54
Automatic Functionality	54
Read Queries	56
Displaying Query Results	58
Create and Update Queries	59
Delete Queries	61
Mixing Active Record and 'Classic' Styles	61
Summary	**62**
Chapter Appendix: MYSQL Query to Set Up 'websites' Database	**63**
Chapter 5: Simplifying HTML Pages and Forms	**67**
Writing a View	**67**
Long and Short PHP Syntax	**69**
Nesting Views	**70**
Practical Issues of Site Architecture	**73**
CI's Form Helper: Entering Data	**74**
Form Helper Advantage One: Clarity	74
Form Helper Advantage Two: Automation	77

My 'Display' Model	**78**
CI's Validation Class: Checking Data Easily	**79**
Set Up Validation	80
Set Up the Controller	81
Set Up the Forms	81
Summary	**83**
Chapter 6: Simplifying Sessions and Security	**85**
Starting to Design a Practical Site with CI	**85**
Moving Around the Site	**86**
Security/Sessions: Using Another CI Library Class	**91**
Turning Sessions into Security	94
Security	**96**
Summary	**98**
Chapter 7: CodeIgniter and Objects	**99**
Object-Oriented Programming	**99**
Working of the CI 'Super-Object'	100
Copying by Reference	103
Adding Your own Code to the CI 'Super-Object'	**105**
Problems with the CI 'Super-Object'	**106**
Summary	**109**
Chapter 8: Using CI to Test Code	**111**
Why Test, and What For?	**111**
CI's Error Handling Class	**113**
CI's Unit Test Class	**115**
When to Use Unit Tests	117
Example of a Unit Test	118
CI's Benchmarking Class	**121**
CI's Profiler Class	**122**
Testing with Mock Databases	**123**
Control and Timing	**124**
Summary	**125**
Chapter 9: Using CI to Communicate	**127**
Using the FTP Class to Test Remote Files	**127**
Machines Talking to Machines Again—XML-RPC	**129**
Getting the XML-RPC Server and Client in Touch with Each Other	131
Formatting XML-RPC Exchanges	132
Debugging	134
Issues with XML-RPC?	135
Talking to Humans for a Change: the Email Class	**136**
Summary	**139**

Chapter 10: How CI Helps to Provide Dynamic Information   141

The Date Helper: Converting and Localizing Dates   142
Working with Text: the Text Helper and Inflector Helper   145
Going International: the Language Class   146
Making HTML Tables the Easy Way: the Table Class   150
Caching Pages   152
Summary   154

Chapter 11: Using CI to Handle Files and Images   155

The File Helper   156
The Download Helper   158
The File Upload Class   160
CI's Image Class   165
Easy File Compression with the CI Zip Class   169
Summary   169

Chapter 12: Production Versions, Updates, and Big Decisions   171

Connections: Check the Config Files   172
    URLs   172
    Databases   172
    Other config Files   173
Look Out for PHP 4/5 and Operating System Differences   173
    Diagnostic Tools   174
Coping with Changes in New CI Versions   177
    How to Load Models, and What to Call Them   178
    How to Initialize Your Own 'library' Classes   179
So Should I Update If a New CI Version Comes Out?   179
How to Add On to CI's Basic Classes   181
Summary   183

Chapter 13: Instant CRUD—or Putting it All Together   185

The CRUD Model: Design Philosophy   186
The Standard Controller Format   187
The Database Tables   189
The Heart of the Model: the Array   189
Function by Function: the CRUD Model   192
    Showall   192
      Reading the Data   195
      Delete and Trydelete   196
    Insert   201
    Insert2   208
    The Test Suite   209
Summary   214

Chapter 14: The Verdict on CI — 215

Some Code: the 'do_test' Model — 216
A Balance Sheet — 225
  Where CI Helped: Structure — 225
  Where CI Helped: Simplicity — 226
  Where CI Helped: Extra Functionality — 226
Problems with CI — 226
  Completeness — 227
  Ease of Use — 227
Summary — 228

Chapter 15: Resources and Extensions — 229

CI's User Forums — 230
Video Tutorials — 232
  Available Plug-ins and Libraries — 232
  AJAX/Javascript — 233
  Authentication — 233
  External Sites — 235
  Comparisons: Which Charting Library to Use? — 235
  CRUD: the Final Frontier — 238
Resources for Other Programmes, e.g. Xampplite, MySQL, PHP — 239
Summary — 240

Index — 241

Preface

This book sets out to explain some of the main features of CI. It doesn't cover them all, or cover any of them in full detail. CI comes with an excellent on-line User Guide that explains most things. This is downloaded with the CI files.

This book doesn't try to duplicate the User Guide. Instead it tries to make it easier for you to pick up how the CI framework works, so you can decide whether it is right for you, and start using it quickly.

In some places, this book goes beyond the User Guide, though, when it tries to explain how CI works. (The User Guide is more practically oriented.) This means that there are some fairly theoretical chapters in between the "here's how" pages. I've found that it helps to understand what CI is doing under the hood; otherwise you sometimes get puzzling error messages that aren't easy to resolve.

I've tried to use a 'real-world' example when showing sections of CI code. I want to show that CI can be used to develop a serious website with a serious purpose. I'm currently running several websites for clients, and I want a program that will monitor them, test them in ways I specify, keep a database of what it has done, and let me have reports when I want them.

The examples in this book don't show it in full detail, of course: but they do, I hope, demonstrate that you can use CI to make pretty well any common coding simpler, and some uncommon stuff as well.

This book steps you through the main features of CodeIgniter in a systematic way, explaining them clearly with illustrative code examples.

What This Book Covers

Chapter 1 explains what CodeIgniter can do, the 'framework', and how CodeIgniter fits in. It further talks about the open-source business model and gives some disadvantages of CodeIgniter, at the end.

Chapter 2 explains what happens when you install the site, and which files will be created. It gives a detailed overview of the required software, and explains the basic configuration of CodeIgniter.

Chapter 3 explains how MVC helps to organize a dynamic website. It goes further to explain the process by which CodeIgniter analyzes an incoming Internet request and decodes which part of your code will handle it. Then CodeIgniter syntax rules and the different types of files or classes you can find—or write for yourself—on a CodeIgniter site are explained. At the end of the chapter, some practical hints on site design are given.

Chapter 4 looks at how you set up a database to work with CodeIgniter, and then how you use the Active Record class to manipulate the database.

Chapter 5 covers various ways of building views, how to create HTML forms quickly, and how to validate your forms using CodeIgniter's validation class.

Chapter 6 looks at one of the basic questions affecting any website i.e. session management and security; we also explore CodeIgniter's session class.

Chapter 7 covers the way in which CodeIgniter uses objects, and the different ways in which you can write and use your own objects.

Chapter 8 covers CodeIgniter classes to help with testing: Unit tests, Benchmarking, the 'profiler' and ways in which CodeIgniter helps you to involve your database in tests without scrambling live data.

Chapter 9 looks at using CodeIgniter's FTP class and email class to make communication easier, and then we venture into Web 2.0 territory using XML-RPC.

Chapter 10 talks about CodeIgniter classes that help in overcoming problems arising regularly when you are building a website, for example, the date helper, the text and inflector helpers, the language class, and the table class.

Chapter 11 looks at several useful CodeIgniter functions and helpers: file helper, download helper, file upload class, image manipulation class, and the ZIP class.

Chapter 12 covers exploring your config files, using diagnostic tools, and potential differences between servers, along with some notes on security.

Chapter 13 shows you how to generalize CRUD operations so that you can do them with two classes: one for the controller, and one for the CRUD model.

Chapter 14 looks at some coding examples, bringing together a lot of the functions that have been discussed bit by bit in the preceding chapters.

Chapter 15 looks at some of the resources available to you when you start to code with CodeIgniter, such as the libraries for AJAX and JavaScript, authentication, charting, and CRUD.

What You Need for This Book

Throughout this book, we will assume that you have the following packages installed and available:

- PHP 4.3.2 or above
- A working web server
- One of MySQL, MySQLi, MS SQL, Postgre, Oracle, SQLite, ODBC

Conventions

In this book, you will find a number of styles of text that distinguish between different kinds of information. Here are some examples of these styles, and an explanation of their meaning.

There are three styles for code. Code words in text are shown as follows: "We can include other contexts through the use of the `include` directive."

A block of code will be set as follows:

```
$active_group = "default";
$db['default']['hostname'] = "";
$db['default']['username'] = "";
$db['default']['password'] = "";
```

When we wish to draw your attention to a particular part of a code block, the relevant lines or items will be made bold:

```
</head>
<body>
<h1 class='test'><?php echo $mytitle; ?> </h1>
<p class='test'><?php echo $mytext; ?> </p>
</body>
```

New terms and **important words** are introduced in a bold-type font. Words that you see on the screen, in menus or dialog boxes for example, appear in our text like this: "clicking the **Next** button moves you to the next screen".

 Warnings or important notes appear in a box like this.

Reader Feedback

Feedback from our readers is always welcome. Let us know what you think about this book, what you liked or may have disliked. Reader feedback is important for us to develop titles that you really get the most out of.

To send us general feedback, simply drop an email to feedback@packtpub.com, making sure to mention the book title in the subject of your message.

If there is a book that you need and would like to see us publish, please send us a note in the **SUGGEST A TITLE** form on www.packtpub.com or email suggest@packtpub.com.

If there is a topic that you have expertise in and you are interested in either writing or contributing to a book, see our author guide on www.packtpub.com/authors.

Customer Support

Now that you are the proud owner of a Packt book, we have a number of things to help you to get the most from your purchase.

Downloading the Example Code for the Book

Visit http://www.packtpub.com/support, and select this book from the list of titles to download any example code or extra resources for this book. The files available for download will then be displayed.

The downloadable files contain instructions on how to use them.

Errata

Although we have taken every care to ensure the accuracy of our contents, mistakes do happen. If you find a mistake in one of our books—maybe a mistake in text or code—we would be grateful if you would report this to us. By doing this you can save other readers from frustration, and help to improve subsequent versions of this book. If you find any errata, report them by visiting http://www.packtpub. com/support, selecting your book, clicking on the **Submit Errata** link, and entering the details of your errata. Once your errata are verified, your submission will be accepted and the errata added to the list of existing errata. The existing errata can be viewed by selecting your title from http://www.packtpub.com/support.

Questions

You can contact us at questions@packtpub.com if you are having a problem with some aspect of the book, and we will do our best to address it.

1
Introduction to CodeIgniter

Most of us just want to write applications that work well, and to do it as simply and easily as we can. This book is about CodeIgniter, a tool for making PHP easier to use.

If you need to produce results, if you think that the details and intricacies of coding are for geeks, then you should look at CodeIgniter (CI to its friends).

CI is free, lightweight, and simple to install, and it really does make your life much easier. Just read this chapter to find out how:

- What CI can do for you
- What is a 'framework' and how does CI fit in?
- The open-source business model
- Some disadvantages of CI (no, it's not perfect)

What can CodeIgniter Do for You?

If you are already writing code in PHP, CodeIgniter will help you to do it better, and more easily. It will cut down on the amount of code you actually type. Your scripts will be easier to read and update. It will help you to give large websites a coherent structure. It will discipline your coding and make it more robust, in some cases without you even knowing it.

That's quite a big claim. You have already spent some time learning PHP, HTML, CSS, a database, and several other acronyms' worth of geek speak. You need a basic, but not necessarily an expert, knowledge of PHP to benefit from CI.

CodeIgniter is not for you if:

- You don't have a reasonable knowledge of PHP and HTML.
- You want to write a basic Content Management System (CMS) quickly and simply, with a minimum of coding. (Look at a product like Expression Engine.)
- You only want to write simple websites with a few standard features.

Save Time

CI doesn't take long to learn, and it quickly pays for your effort in the time saved later on. Let's look at a simple measure:

How CI cuts down the amount of code you need to type.

This is not just good for the lazy. The less you type, the fewer mistakes you make, and the less time you spend debugging your code. The smaller your code is, the faster it loads and less space it takes up.

Here are two examples (which are explained later on in this book, so don't worry now about how they work!).

Imagine you are writing a database query. This is how you might write a function within your PHP programme to query a MySQL database:

```
$connection = mysql_connect("localhost","fred","12345");
 mysql_select_db("websites", $connection);
 $result = mysql_query ("SELECT * FROM sites", $connection);
 while ($row = mysql_fetch_array($result, MYSQL_NUM))
 {
    foreach ($row as $attribute)
       print "{$attribute[1]} ";
 }
```

Now see how a CI function would handle a similar query:

```
$this->load->database('websites');
$query = $this->db->get('sites');
   foreach ($query->result() as $row)
   {
      print $row->url
   }
```

Compare the character counts: 244 for the traditional syntax; 112 for CI.

Now let's imagine that you are writing a data entry form in HTML, and you want a drop-down query box. Let's say this drop-down query box shows three options and allows the user to select one of them. In HTML, a drop-down box can be created like this:

```
<select name="type">
<option value="1">www.this.com</option>
<option value="2">www.that.com</option>
<option value="3" selected>www.theother.com</option>
</select>
```

CI's version is both shorter and, because it works from an array, more adapted to PHP processing:

```
$urlarray = array(
                '1'  => 'www.this.com',
                '2'  => 'www.that.com',
                '3'  => 'www.theother.com',
            );

$variable .= form_dropdown('url', $urlarray, '1');
```

In HTML, you need to type 154 characters; in CI, 128.

Make Your Site More Robust

Although you don't need to write as much code, CI provides a lot of the standard functionality for you, and remembers all those oddities and quirks. It keeps track of things you may have forgotten all about. (Those little touches that distinguish amateur sites from professional ones…)

Keep Your Links Up-To-Date Automatically

Imagine that you've just written a menu page, with lots of hyperlinks to other pages in your site. They are all in the traditional HTML format:

```
<a href="http://www.mysite.com/index.php/start/hello/fred
">say hello to Fred</a>
```

Then, you decide to move the site to another URL. That means you have to go painstakingly through your code, looking for each URL, and re-writing it, or else none of your links will work.

CI gives you a simple function to write hyperlinks like this:

```
echo anchor(start/hello/fred, Say hello to Fred);
```

CI also encourages you to put the URL of your site in a configuration file that the rest of your site can access. CI's anchor function that we've used here automatically refers to that configuration file. So, when you come to move your site, you only need to change that one entry in the configuration file, and all your hyperlinks update automatically.

Save Database Crashes: 'prep' Your Data Entry Forms

Data entry is fraught with problems. Because of limitations of HTML and databases, data that contain certain symbols— for example, apostrophes and quotation marks— may cause your database to crash or to give results you did not expect.

The answer to this is to prepare or 'prep' your data in your data entry form, before it is submitted to the database. All this takes time and a certain amount of extra coding.

CI's form helper does this, automatically. So, when you create an input box by typing:

```
echo form_input('username', 'johndoe');
```

You're also getting the hidden benefit of:

```
function form_prep($str = '')
{
    if ($str === '')
    {
        return '';
    }

    $temp = '__TEMP_AMPERSANDS__';

    // Replace entities to temporary markers so that
    // htmlspecialchars won't mess them up
    $str = preg_replace("/&#(\d+);/", "$temp\\1;", $str);
    $str = preg_replace("/&(\w+);/",  "$temp\\1;", $str);

    $str = htmlspecialchars($str);

    // In case htmlspecialchars misses these.
    $str = str_replace(array("'", '"'), array("&#39;",
                                    "&quot;"), $str);

    // Decode the temp markers back to entities
    $str = preg_replace("/$temp(\d+);/","&#\\1;",$str);
    $str = preg_replace("/$temp(\w+);/","&\\1;",$str);

    return $str;
}
```

This is code that handles special characters like '&'; so that they don't cause confusion while your form is being submitted. As you can see, there is some quite tricky regex code in there.

Possibly you like typing out regexes. Some people like lying on beds of nails, some like listening to ABBA; it's a free country. (Well, it is where I'm writing this.) But if you don't like these things, you can let CI do them for you (the regexes, I mean, not ABBA), and you needn't even be aware of the code that's working away in the background for you, every time you write that one simple line of code:

```
echo form_input('username', 'johndoe');
```

Make Your Code Bolder

CI also makes it easy to do things you might not have tried before. Of course, PHP users can always integrate libraries from PEAR and other sources, but these aren't always easy to integrate, or use, and their syntax and standards differ greatly. CI has a common set of standards, and once you've mastered its syntax, all its parts work together without complication. All its code is well-written and reliable, and is tested out by its user community. It puts much more sophistication in your hands.

Let's look at two examples to illustrate this point.

Send Email Attachments without Hassles

Sending emails is a complex business. CI's code for doing it looks easy to follow:

```
$this->load->library('email');
$this->email->from('your@your-site.com', 'Your Name');
$this->email->subject('Email Test');
$this->email->message('Testing the email class.');
$this->email->send();
```

There are a number of issues involved in sending emails: setting word-wrapping (and escaping it so long URLs don't get wrapped and broken up) for example, or sending attachments. The standard PHP functions can get quite complex here, and the result is that many code writers are tempted to avoid using these functions if they possibly can.

CI's email class makes it simple to send an attachment. You write:

```
$this->email->attach('/path/to/photo1.jpg');
```

CI does the rest. Working behind the scenes, for example, is a function that sorts out MIME types for nearly hundred different types of attachment. So it knows that your photo, photo1.jpg, is an 'image/jpeg' MIME type. It remembers to generate boundary delimiters in the right places around your attachments. It takes care of wrapping your text, and it allows you to easily mark out chunks of text you don't want wrapped.

Save Bandwidth by Zipping Files That Users Need to Download

To save bandwidth, it's a fairly common practice to compress or 'ZIP' files before you download them. That's not something I've ever done, and I wouldn't know how to go about it. On the other hand, CI has a nice facility that allows you to produce zipped files with four lines of code:

```
$name = 'mydata1.txt';
$data = 'the contents of my file............';
$this->zip->add_data($name, $data);
$this->zip->archive('c:/my_backup.zip');
```

Run this, and you find a ZIP archive on your C drive containing one file. Your ZIP filer reader will unzip it and produce the original data for you.

People who use your site won't know that you've produced this impressive result so easily. They'll be impressed! Your site will save bandwidth. You did it in minutes rather than hours.

Yes, But…What is CodeIgniter? What are Frameworks?

Shortly after programming was invented, someone noticed that it involved many repetitive operations. And shortly after that, someone else — maybe it was Ada Lovelace, spanner in hand, adjusting Babbage's differential engine, or maybe it was Alan Turing at Bletchley Park — decided to modularize code, so you only had to write certain chunks once, and could then re-use them. PHP programmers are used to writing separate chunks of code in functions, and then storing those functions in `include` files.

At one level, a framework is just that: lots of chunks of code, stored in separate files, which simplify the coding of repetitive operations.

In the examples above, connecting to the database or building HTML form elements are abstracted and simplified for you. You call a function in the framework, which is easier to handle than the original code.

It goes beyond that. Writing code involves continuous choices between the many ways of tackling the same problem; so most frameworks also impose a set of choices on you. They've started to handle the problem one way, so you have to go that way as well. If these are sensible choices, this makes your life much simpler too. (If not, it's like trying to write a sales brochure using Excel, or do cash-flow projections using Word. Both can probably be done, but neither is the best use of your time.)

Sensible design decisions make sure that the things you need are accessible, but prevent them from spilling over into each other. A good framework makes those decisions for you, starting you off with a sensible foundation for your program and guiding you through the next steps.

Mention frameworks nowadays, and people think of *Ruby on Rails*.

Rails has become the success story of the last year or so, because it apparently offers effortless and rapid website development, with a minimum amount of coding. Essentially, it is a structure and a set of tools, built for use with the Ruby language, that allow you to build certain types of Ruby programs more quickly. It's not the only framework for Ruby, but it is very effective and, deservedly, very popular. On the other hand, if you have put in the time and effort to learn PHP, starting over again in Ruby is a long haul.

There are several frameworks available for PHP as well. CI is only one of about 40. They include the Zend framework, Cake, Trax, and others. There's a handy chart at `http://www.phpit.net/article/ten-different-php-frameworks/` that compares ten of the most popular.

If you look at them, you'll notice that postings on their user forums get very heated about which framework is the best. The truth seems to be that each has its strengths, and none is without its own weaknesses. My touchstone is that I'm busy; so frameworks should save me time, and having found one that works for me, I am sticking to it. That's why this book is just about CI.

And Who is That Man?

CI was written by Rick Ellis, rock musician turned programmer. Rick makes his living as CEO of pMachine, which sells an excellent content management system called *Expression Engine*. In January 2006, he wrote on his blog, `http://www.ellislab.com`:

"... I spent a couple weeks researching and installing PHP frameworks, really banging on quite a few of them, and I was absolutely dismayed. I discovered that most frameworks suffer from these problems:

- They have horrid, terrible documentation, if it exists at all.

- They make an endless number of assumptions regarding your knowledge and skill level, and generally expect you to figure it all out.

- They are written for people who have root server privileges and can change system settings.

- They assume that you have access to the command line. In fact, many do not work if you can't bash out commands.

- They tend to require lots of dependencies, like the PEAR libraries or various open source ones.

- They tend to be needlessly complex to use, with obtuse syntax, XML based templates, and other features that are simply not necessary for most web applications.

- They are either ponderously big, or too minimalist to be useful.

- The most current frameworks only run on PHP 5, which at present only has a 5% adoption rate.

I have yet to find a single PHP framework that is truly, really, actually simple to use, is thoroughly documented from top to bottom, natively includes all the tools needed to build robust applications, has a browser-based interface, and is designed for your average PHP coder, without admin privileges, who uses a standard hosting account. Not one. Which leads me to think there's a market for just such a product. ..."

The result was CI, written as a spare time project. Rick generously decided to make it available, free of charge. In between running his business, he also updates CI from time to time. He's also created an excellent forum, where CI users can raise issues and share tips, as well as finding (and sometimes solving) bugs in his code. All this is available on the CI website at `http://www.codeigniter.com/`.

Did he meet his own objectives? Read on and judge for yourself...

The 'Open Source' Business Model

There can be something disconcerting about this sort of software. If you like your software with expensive support contracts and a 'big company' name, then CI is not for you. (But then, what are you doing using PHP, anyway? PHP users know that support, and the development of PHP software, depends partly on the unpaid efforts of the 'community'—hundreds or thousands of users.)

There are some problems with community support. Consistency and high quality are not 'guaranteed'—anyone can post to the forum, and sometimes these postings are just plain wrong. (Note that if you read the small print on the licence for expensive commercial software, quality isn't guaranteed there either.) But with 'open source' products, you do have to take an intelligent interest rather than accepting everything you read on forums at face value. CI is a framework for people who are able to take an intelligent interest.

However, any sensible developer has to wonder if it's wise to invest time and energy in a product that is a 'one man band'. Rick Ellis wrote it as a spare time project, with some help from his pMachine colleague Paul Burdick. It's free. He makes no commitment to maintain it or develop it. He might go back to being a rock musician.

On the other hand, once you've downloaded it, the version you downloaded will continue to work. You don't have to rely on upgrades and patches. Rick's coding is excellent and there have been few serious bugs in it. If it works for you, then there is no reason why it shouldn't continue to work. So far I've only found two cases in which my code failed to work, and the fault was a bug in the framework rather than in my own coding on top of it. (Both bugs have since been solved.)

The CI website is the gateway to the community and forums.

What CI Doesn't Do

There are some things that CI doesn't do. Rick intended CI to be a small and 'lightweight' framework. (The zipped download for version 1.5 is only 737 KB and downloads in seconds. The Zend framework is 10 megabytes.) It's not the answer to all the problems you will ever have. But it does:

- Make it easier and quicker to programme in PHP
- Structure your site and help you through the architectural decisions.

One result of being 'lightweight' is that it does not have as many features as some of its rivals. Rails has achieved prominence partly because it contains 'scaffolding' and 'generators'. These are tools that automatically write certain basic scripts for you. So, for example, once you have set up a database, Rails creates 'out-of-the-box' web pages to do basic Create, Read, Update, and Delete (CRUD) operations on the database tables.

In addition, Rails allows you to write 'generators'—pieces of code that automatically write other basic scripts. The Rails community has created quite a lot of these; so you can automatically generate scripts that do all sorts of clever things.

CI doesn't do this. (There is rudimentary 'scaffolding'—scaffolds are templates that describe how the application database maybe used— in CI, but as the online manual puts it: "Scaffolding is intended for development use only. It provides very little security…. If you use scaffolding make sure you disable it immediately after you are through using it. DO NOT leave it enabled on a live site." Enough said.)

Instead CI concentrates on making basic things easy. Some of the things it handles are:

- Session management and cookies (see Chapter 6)
- Database access and queries (see Chapter 4)
- Building HTML stuff, like pages and forms, and validating form entries (see Chapter 5)
- Testing (Chapter 8)
- Communicating on the Internet, using FTP or XMLRPC (Chapter 9)

Sound familiar? All of these are basic processes, which you will have to go through if you're building a dynamic website. CI makes these processes easier, and makes your code more likely to work.

License

If you are building a commercial application, the license terms for any software you are using become critical. (If you are raising venture capital, expect the VC's lawyers to go over them in detail.) No problems with CI. It has a very generous licence that is downloaded with your files.

Unlike some commercial software I could think of, CI's license even fits on one screen. Here it is, in the following screenshot:

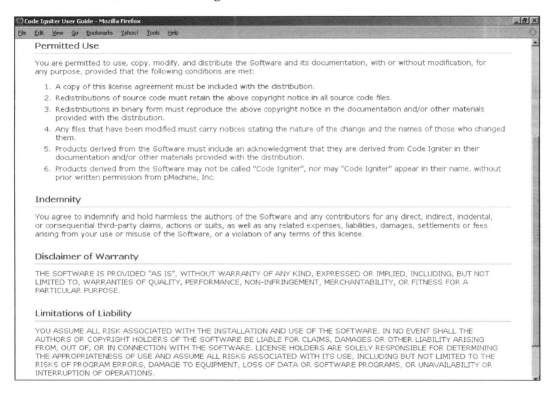

Summary

If you already know some PHP and are writing intelligent websites, the CodeIgniter framework is all about making your life easier. It helps you

- Save time
- Make your site more robust
- Achieve more sophisticated coding

It makes coding fun again, rather than a chore.

There are quite a few frameworks, and not just for the PHP language. All of them offer you chunks of pre-written code that make the repetitive or complex processes of coding easier, and impose a helpful structure on your site development.

This book does not make any comparisons between frameworks. I've found CI works for me, and I want to explain how and why. I hope that's useful to you, and that you will be able to save as much time as I did, and enjoy the coding process more, as a result.

This book takes you through some of the framework's main features, and tries to explain some of what goes on 'under the hood'.

I've used a real-world example for the code illustrations in this book to try to show that CI is a serious tool that can be quickly and easily used in a demanding environment.

Enjoy!

2
Two Minutes' Work: Setting up a CodeIgniter Site

Setting up the CI package on your web server is easy. This small chapter explains what happens when you install the site, and which files will be created. Let's look at:

- What software you require for your development site
- Installing the CI files: a simple download and unzip operation
- The basic configuration of CI: what the folders are and how they are organized
- The initial controller and view that CI installs
- Some basic modifications to show how these work

Prerequisites

CodeIgniter is very flexible. It will work equally well with PHP 4.3.2 and above, or PHP 5. Since the majority of ISPs still don't support PHP 5, this is useful, and keeps down the hosting costs.

You will also need a database. CI's online user guide says: "Supported databases are MySQL, MySQLi, MS SQL, Postgre, Oracle, SQLite, and ODBC."

In order to develop and test a dynamic website, you need a web server. Normally, you would develop and test your site on a local server, i.e., one that runs on your own machine (with the loopback address **127.0.0.1** or **localhost**) rather than on a remote site on the Internet.

If you aren't familiar with the process of setting up a web server, it's easiest to install a package such as **Xampplite**, which installs Apache, PHP, and MySQL on to a Windows machine with minimum configuration by you. Xampplite is free, comes with comprehensive instructions, and is almost always easy to install. Alternatively, some versions of Windows come with their own web server.

It also helps to have a good PHP editor on your system. You can do it all on a text editor, but I find that the syntax highlighting feature of a good editor saves me from making lots of simple mistakes with unclosed brackets or mismatched quotation marks.

Once you've reached this far, I estimate it will take you two minutes to have CI running on your system.

Installing CodeIgniter

One thing you don't need is your credit card: CI is completely free!

Once your server is set up, go to the CodeIgniter site at `http://www.codeigniter.com/` and download the latest version of the framework. Version 1.5.3, the latest, is only 737KB when zipped, so the download doesn't take that long

Unzip the folder, and install the CodeIgniter files in your web root folder. If you are using Xampplite, this is usually the `htdocs` folder within the `Xampplite` folder.

The CodeIgniter `index.php` file should be in the root directory. The root folder is the folder that you would point at if you navigated to the site—in this case, by accessing `http://127.0.0.1`. Of the two minutes we need to set up the site, one minute is up!

Included with CI is a comprehensive user guide (in the `user_guide` folder). You'll use this a lot. It is usually clear, and often goes into more detail than this book can. So, try it if you get stuck.

When these files are on your machine, you can access them in two ways:

- As a URL—e.g., `http://127.0.0.1`
- Through the normal directory path: e.g.,
  `C:/xampplite/htdocs/index.php`

You should be able to see the CI welcome screen by simply navigating to your URL with the browser. It's that simple! The welcome page tells you that what you are seeing is built by two files, a view and a controller.

Exploring the File Structure

Once you have installed the CI files, have a look at the new directories that have been created. Understanding what the different types of files do is critical.

Your root folder should now look something like the diagram below. If you've ever looked at Rails, this structure will look fairly familiar.

You can divide these folders into three groups:

- The ones you will populate (e.g., controllers, models, and views: all in the `application` folder). Apart from the welcome view and controller that you have just seen, these folders are empty.

- The files in the `system` folder are the system code for CI (`system/libraries`, `system/codeigniter`, `system/drivers`, etc.). You can read them, and alter them if you wish—but don't do this until you understand how CI works. And if you alter the base code, remember that you may have to alter it again when you download an update of CodeIgniter, since the new version may overwrite your alterations. You may also find that the new code no longer works with your amendments. Lastly, you may find that what Rick wrote is pretty good as it is.

- The ones that are half written already, but may need additions or changes (`language`, `config`, `errors`.) These folders are set to defaults, but you will need to alter your `config` files right away; so let's get that over with.

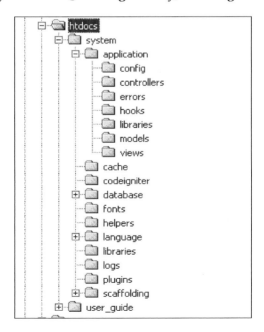

The Configuration File

Remember we were going to take two minutes to set our site up? The second minute is spent doing some basic configuration.

The `config` folder contains a group of files that set basic configurations for your site. Open the `config/config.php` file and tell the site where to find itself. The first few lines of the file should say something like:

```
/*
|--------------------------------------------------
| Base Site URL
|--------------------------------------------------
|
| URL to your Code Igniter root. Typically this
| will be your base URL, WITH a trailing slash:
|
|   http://www.your-site.com/
|
*/
$config['base_url'] = "http://127.0.0.1/";
/*
```

Notice how well CI files are commented!

Alter the values in quotes to match your own web root. If you have a problem, more detailed setup instructions are given in the online manual.

As a basic principle, use the `config.php` file to store information about your site rather than scattering it around your files. Firstly, it is easier to update if it's all in one place. Secondly, when you transfer your site from the development server to the production server, you'll only have to make only one set of changes. Lastly, many CI functions assume that certain information is to be found there.

There are other `config` files in the `config` folder, but you can safely leave them at their default settings for now.

Of the two minutes we needed to set up the site that was the second one. In the rest of this chapter, we'll play around with our site.

Does it Work?

The easy way to see if your site is working is to navigate to it using your browser. Assuming you're running it in the root folder of a local server, type in `http://127.0.0.1` and you should see this:

That means CI is up and running. Did it take you more than two minutes?

Summary

In this chapter, we've seen how easy it is to install CI. Once you have a development web server set up, all you need to do is download the CI code, unzip it, and copy it over.

Then, we looked quickly at the shape of the files we've installed and did some basic configuration, and there we were: a working CI site.

If this chapter is disappointingly short, it's because CI is easy to install. Like everything else in this book, it's about saving time and making life easier.

3
Navigating Your Site

Now that we've installed CI, we need to understand how it works.

Readers familiar with design patterns will have recognized by now that CI implements the Model—View—Controller (MVC) pattern. This is a method of organizing the files that make up a website, or, if you like, of splitting the site into sensible parts rather than having one huge lump of code.

In this chapter, we'll look briefly at the theory behind MVC, and then at the way CI organizes itself internally. In particular, what goes in those different folders and how do they communicate? How is a site structured? And how does CI navigate around it?

This chapter looks at:

- How MVC helps to organize a dynamic website
- The process by which CI analyzes an incoming Internet request and decides which part of your code will handle it
- What the code does then
- CodeIgniter syntax rules
- The different types of files or classes you can find—or write for yourself—on a CI site
- How to pass parameters to controllers using the URL
- How to write better views and pass dynamic data to them
- How a reply is returned to the surfer
- How the files or classes pass information and control to each other
- How useful code is kept inside helper and library files
- Some practical hints on site design.

MVC—Just Another Acronym?

MVC is a means of organizing a dynamic website. The design pattern has been around since 1979 when it was first described by the Norwegian, Trygve Reenskaug. Here's an outline of the different types of files:

- Models are objects, which represent the underlying data. They hover above the database and access it as required. They can also perform operations on data to add meaning to it.

- Views show the state of the model. They are responsible for displaying information to the end user. (Although they are normally HMTL views, they might be any form of interface. They might be views specially adapted for small PDA screens or WAP telephones, for example.)

- Controllers offer options to change the state of the model. They are responsible for consulting models. They provide the dynamic data to views.

CI has subfolders for `models`, `views`, and `controllers`. Each file within them is a `.php` file, usually in the form of a class that follows certain naming conventions.

CI helps you to follow the MVC pattern, and as a result makes it much easier to lay your code out. CI allows you a lot of flexibility, and you get all the advantages of the MVC structure.

Try to think in MVC terms as you write. As far as possible, try to keep your 'views' focused purely on presentation, and your 'controllers' purely on controlling application flow. Keep the application logic in the data models and the database.

This way, if you do decide to create a new set of views for a new display method, you don't have to alter much code in any of the controllers or the models. If you update some of your 'business logic', you only have to change code in the models.

On the other hand, while this is a very interesting and useful division, it's important not to take it too seriously. MVC is intended to help you and not to be a straitjacket. Different programs and frameworks implement MVC in slightly different ways. The CI forums contain many anguished queries about the 'right' way to implement MVC. (Should I do database queries from controllers, or should this only be done in models? Can I return a view directly from a model, or should I go through a controller first?)

Rather than trying to achieve the theoretically 'right' result, just keep in mind the two useful principles. These are set out in the *Design and Architectural Goals* section of CI's User Guide:

- **Loose Coupling**: Coupling is the degree to which the components of a system rely on each other. The less the components depend on each other, the more re-usable and flexible the system becomes. Our goal was a very loosely coupled system.

- **Component Singularity**: Singularity is the degree to which components have a narrowly focused purpose. In CodeIgniter, each class and its functions are highly autonomous in order to allow maximum usefulness.

These were Rick Ellis's objectives in building CI, and they are good objectives for your own sites too. Provided that you meet these objectives, it doesn't matter very much what your code sections are called.

It does work. My own experience is that 'loose coupled' helpers or libraries written for one site can be very easily dropped in to another, saving hours of development time.

So, if your controller queries the database directly, or your model calls a view, the CI code will work properly—there's usually no technical issue—but your MVC interpretation may not be 'correct'. Don't worry, be happy!

The Structure of a CI Site: Controllers and Views

Your entire CI site is dynamic. That is, there are probably no 'static' pages that you can look at as simple HTML code. (You can add some if you wish, but they'll be outside the CI framework.) So, where is your site?

When we installed CI, we noticed that the `application` folder includes subfolders called `models`, `views`, and `controllers`. Each response that a CI site produces is assembled by these three types of files.

Let's look at the process in detail.

To emphasize the point that we are not dealing with static pages, each with its own URL, we will show you the 'URL' request and show how CI interprets it. First of all, consider a normal Internet request. A connection is made to the URL of your site, `www.example.com`, and then through the socket comes an HTTP request like:

```
GET /folder/file.html HTTP/1.0
```

GET is the type of request, HTTP/1.0 is the version of HTTP being used, and everything in between is the relative path, and name of your file. But on your site, there are no simple static HTML files to be found. Instead, all incoming requests are intercepted by the index.php file.

If the user is requesting a page on your site with the correct URL—say by clicking on a hyperlink on one of your pages—the request will look more like this:

```
GET /index.php/tests/showall HTTP/1.0
```

If the user doesn't know the exact URL and just requests www.example.com, then CI has a system for setting a default address (We'll see how to do that in a moment.). In either case, the steps are:

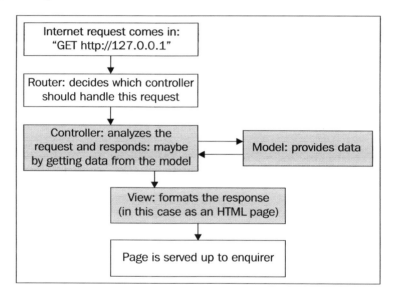

A request coming in from the Internet to your web root is intercepted by the index.php file, which acts as a 'router'. That is, it calls a 'controller', which then returns a 'view'.

How does the router know which controller to call? As we've seen, sometimes the incoming request tells it. For instance, if the request says:

```
GET http://127.0.0.1/index.php/welcome/index
```

and if you have a controller called welcome, that's where the request goes.

The Welcome Controller

So, let's look at the `welcome` controller. It's the one controller that has already been written and the code is at `system/application/controllers/welcome.php`. Here's what it says:

```php
<?php
  class  Welcome extends Controller
  {
        function Welcome()
        {
                parent::Controller();
        }
        function index()
        {
              $this->load->view('welcome_message');
        }

  }
?>
```

You'll see from the second line that this file is a class. Every controller inherits from an original `Controller` class—hence `extends Controller`. Within the class are two functions or methods—`Welcome()` and `index()`.

> CI requires controller names to start with an uppercase letter (`class Welcome`), though the file is saved as `/system/application/controllers/welcome.php`—the same name but with a lowercase letter.

The next three lines make up the constructor function. Notice that CI uses the older PHP 4 convention for naming constructor functions, which is also acceptable on PHP 5—it doesn't require you to use PHP 5 and is happy with either version of the language. The constructor function is used to set up the class each time you instantiate it. In here, you put any instructions to load other libraries or models, or any definitions of class variables.

So far the only thing inside the constructor is the `parent::Controller()` statement. This is just way of making sure that you inherit the functionality of the `Controller` class. If you want to understand the parent CI `Controller` class in detail, you can look at the file `/system/libraries/controller.php`.

(One of the reassuring things about CI is that all the code is there for you to inspect, though you don't often need to.)

Working with Views

Let's go back to the incoming request for a moment. The router needs to know, not only which controller should handle the request, but also which function within that controller. That is why the request is specified GET http://127.0.0.1/welcome/ index. So the router looks for a function inside the welcome controller called index. And here it is!

Then comes the index() function. This function simply loads a view ('welcome_view') using CI's loader function (this->load->view). At this stage, it doesn't do anything cool with the view, such as passing it dynamic information. That comes later.

The 'welcome_view' it wants to load is in the views folder that you have just installed: system/application/views/welcome_view.php. This particular view is only a simple HTML page, but it is saved as a PHP file because most views have PHP code in them. (No point in doing all this if we're only going to serve up plain old static HTML.)

Here's the (slightly shortened) code for the view:

```
<html>
<head>
  <title>Welcome to Code Igniter</title>
  <style type="text/css">
    body
    {
     background-color: #fff;
     margin: 40px;
     font-family: Lucida Grande, Verdana, Sans-serif;
     font-size: 14px;
     color: #4F5155;
    }
. . . . . more style information here . . . .
  </style>
</head>
<body>

  <h1>Welcome to Code Igniter!</h1>

  <p>The page you are looking at is being generated dynamically by
     Code Igniter.</p>
```

```
<p>If you would like to edit this page you'll find it located at:</p>
<code>system/application/views/welcome_message.php</code>

<p>The corresponding controller for this page is found at:</p>
<code>system/application/controllers/welcome.php</code>

<p>If you are exploring Code Igniter for the very first time, you
should start by reading the <a href="user_guide/">User
Guide</a>.</p>
</body>
</html>
```

As you can see, it consists entirely of HTML, with an embedded CSS stylesheet. In this simple example, the controller hasn't passed any variables to the view.

The Default Controller

I mentioned earlier that CI routes requests to a default controller if the request doesn't specify where it wants to go. You set the default controller from a `config` file—in this case it's `/system/application/config/routes`. This contains:

```
$route['default_controller'] = "welcome";
```

If you don't set a default, the site users who don't know the exact URL to request—that's most of them, when you think about it—will get '404 not found' pages.

In this case, the default route is to your `welcome` controller.

If no function is specified, the route defaults to the `/index` function of whatever controller is selected, so make sure you include an `index` function, if only to prevent '404' pages. Please note that the `index` function is not the same as the constructor function.

You can alter this default if you like, by including in the controller(s) you want to alter, a function called `_remap($function)`, where `$function` is the function you want to intercept and redirect. `_remap` always gets called first, whatever the URL says.

CodeIgniter Syntax Rules

Before we start, let's just summarize the syntax rules that CI uses. The framework expects files to be set out in certain ways, otherwise it may have difficulty indentifying your files properly, or using them.

Controller

This is a class (i.e. OO code). It is called directly by the URL, e.g., `'www.example.com/index.php/start/hello'`. Controllers are used to call functions by name, e.g., `mainpage()`; however, you cannot call functions inside another controller.

Syntax: Controllers begin with `class Start extends Controller` (where the name of the controller has the first letter in uppercase) and are saved as a `.php` file in the `/system/application/controllers` folder. When saved, they should not have the first letter in uppercase; as in `start.php` and not `Start.php`. Also, they should include constructor containing at least:

```
function display()
  {parent::Controller();}
```

All other code must be written as separate functions within the class e.g., `hello()` function

View

Views are HTML files that can contain PHP 'islands'. They are loaded by `$this->load->view('testview', $data)`. Loading and using the view are done in the same action.

Syntax: The view is written in HTML. The PHP code is included within `<?php ?>` tags as with any HTML file. It is saved as a `.php` file in the `views` folder.

Types of Files or Classes on a CI Site

There are several different sub-folders within the `application` folder. We have already looked at the `controller`, `config`, and `views` folders.

But what are libraries, models, and scripts? This is one area where CI seems rather confusing. (If you have used versions of CI before version 1.5, you'll realize why. Rick Ellis wasn't happy with the earlier versions and has changed the structure quite a lot. However, for compatibility reasons, some anomalies remain.)

In a technical sense, these folders are treated in much the same way. There's no reason why you shouldn't put your code in any of these folders, though you'll have to make it slightly different in each.

Let's say that you have written a block of code called `display`, for example, which contains a function called `mainpage`. There are four ways you might have done this: as a model, a library, a helper, or a plug-in. The following table summarizes the differences between each approach, and shows you how to load and use each type.

File type	How to use it
model	This is a class (i.e. it's object-oriented or OO code)
	Load it like this: `$this->load->model('display');`
	Use it like this: `$this->display->mainpage();`
	Notes on syntax:

	It must begin with `class Display extends Model`
	It must include a constructor containing at least:
	  `function display()`
	    `{parent::Model();}`

	and contain a separate `mainpage()` function.
	Conceptually: The User Guide says, "Models are PHP classes that are designed to work with information in your database."
library	It is present in both the `system` and the `application` folder. Again, this is a class. (Note: your own libraries are not automatically included in the CI super-object, so you need to call CI resources in a different way. See Chapter 7 for details)
	Load it like this: `$this->load->library('display');`
	Use it like this: `$this->display->mainpage();`
	Notes on syntax: No need to extend a base class, or for a constructor function. This is enough:

	`class Display()`
	`{`
	`    function mainpage()`
	`    { //code here    }`
	`}`

	Conceptually: Intended to hold your own code to extend CI functionality, or to create site-specific functionality.
helper	It can be in the `system/helpers` folder or in an `application/helpers` folder. This is a script (procedural code, not an OO class)
	Load it like this: `$this->load->helper('display');`
	Use a function from it like this: `mainpage();`
	Notes on syntax:
	The file should be saved as `display_helper.php`—i.e., add `_helper` to the file name.
	`mainpage()` should be a function included in the file, which is simply a collection of separate functions, not a class. As a result you can't directly access CI's other resources any more.
	Conceptually: 'helpers' are intended as a collection of low-level functions to help you perform specific tasks.

File type	How to use it
plug-in	It is present in the `system/plugins` folder but can also be created in an `applications/plugins` folder. This is a script (not an OO class)
	Load it like this: `$this->load->plugin('display');`
	Use a function from it like this: `mainpage();`
	Notes on syntax: The file should be saved as `display_pi.php`—i.e. add `_pi` to end of filename.
	`mainpage()` should be a function included in the file, which is simply a collection of separate functions, not a class. As a result, you can't directly access CI's other resources any more.
	Conceptually: The User Guide says, "…the main difference is that a plug-in usually provides a single function, whereas a Helper is usually a collection of functions….. plug-ins are intended to be created and shared by our community." (See Chapter 15 for an example plug-in.)

You could put your piece of new code in any of these folders, though you'd have to write it as an object-oriented class in the first two, and as a procedural script in the second, and in the latter case, you wouldn't be able to draw directly on other CI classes. Otherwise, the difference between the types of folder is largely a conceptual one.

You'll notice that CI can have two sets of helpers, plug-ins, and libraries, though not of models. There can be one set of each in the `application` folder, and another set in the `system` folder. The difference, again, is largely conceptual.

- Those in the `system` folder are intended to be part of the core CI code and to be shared by all applications. If you update to a later version of CI, then you will overwrite the `system` folder and these files may be modified.

- Those in the `application` folder will only to be available to that one application. If you update to a new version of CI, the `application` folder will not be overwritten.

- When you try to load a helper, plug-in, or library, CI sensibly looks in both paths. If you attempt to load a library called `display`, for example, CI will look first in your `system/application/libraries` directory. If the directory does not exist or the `display` library is not there, CI will then look in the `system/libraries` folder.

- This means that it is possible to effectively over-write CI's core libraries, helpers, and plug-ins by introducing your own with the same names in the `applications` folder. Don't do this accidentally. However, this flexibility is a great advantage for experienced CI users if you want to extend the basic classes and scripts that come with CI—see Chapter 13.

What are All Those Folders For?

Now that we've looked at the key types of folder in some detail, here is a reference table of the structure of a CI site.

application	config	Configuration files: hold basic information about your site that persists between sessions
	controllers	Controllers
	errors	Contains templates for error announcements. You may never need to touch these.
	hooks	Empty when first installed, use this for any 'hooks' you create. Hooks are a way of controlling the way other files load.
	libraries	Collections of your code, intended to work with this specific application
	models	Collections of your code, again intended to work with this specific application
	views	Templates for showing information to the user
cache		Empty when first installed: if you enable caching (see Chapter 10) data is stored here
codeigniter		Basic system files.
database		Library files for CI's database class.
fonts		Not explained in the user guide, except as a place to store fonts for watermarking images
helpers		System level 'helpers'
language		You can store your own lists of key phrases here—see Chapter 11
libraries		System level libraries
logs		If you set the system to log errors, log files are created here by default
plugins		More system-level code blocks
scaffolding		System-level library to enable rudimentary 'scaffolding'.

Designing a Better View

At this stage, you might ask why we are going through so much effort to serve up a simple HTML page. Why not put everything in one file? For a simple site, that's a valid point—but whoever heard of a simple site? One of the coolest things about CI is the way it helps us to develop a consistent structure, so that as we add to and develop our site, it is internally consistent, well laid out, and simple to maintain.

At the start, we need three common steps:

- Write a view page
- Write a stylesheet
- Update our `config` file to specify where the stylesheet is

After this is done, we need to update our controller to accept parameters from the URL, and pass variables to the view.

First, let's redesign our view and save it as:
`system/application/views/testview.php`.

```html
<html>
<head>
  <!DOCTYPE html PUBLIC '-//W3C//DTD XHTML 1.0
  Strict//EN'http:\/\/www.w3.org/TR/xhtml1/DTD/xhtml1-strict.dtd'>
  <html xmlns='http:\/\/www.w3.org/1999/xhtml'>
  <title>Web test Site</title>
  <base href= <?php echo "$base"; ?> >
  <link rel="stylesheet" type="text/css" href="<?php echo
  "$base/$css";?>">
</head>
<body>
  <h1><?php echo $mytitle; ?> </h1>
  <p class='test'> <?php echo $mytext; ?> </p>
</body>
</html>
```

It's still mostly HTML, but notice the PHP 'code islands' in the highlighted lines.

You'll notice that the first bits of PHP code build in a link to a stylesheet. Let's save a simple stylesheet as `mystyles.css`, in the site's root folder. It just says:

```css
h1 {
margin: 5px;
padding-left: 10px;
padding-right: 10px;
background: #ffffff;
color: blue;
width: 100%;
font-size: 36px;
}
.test{
margin: 5px;
padding-left: 10px;
padding-right: 10px;
```

```
background: #ffffff;
color: red;
width: 100%;
font-size: 36px;
}
```

That gives us two styles to play with, and you'll see we've used them both in the view.

Firstly, let's add an entry to the `config` file:

```
$config['css'] = "mystyles.css";
```

This is simply to tell the site the name and address of the CSS file that we've just written.

But note that the link to the stylesheet is referenced at `$base/$css`—where do those variables `$base` and `$css`, get their values? And come to think of it, those variables `$mytitle` and `$mytext` at the end of the code? We need a new controller!

Designing a Better Controller

Now, we need a new controller. We'll call it `Start` and save it as `/system/ application/controllers/start.php`.

This controller has to do several things:

- Call a view
- Provide the view with the base URL and the location of the `css` file we just wrote
- Provide the view with some data: it's expecting a title (`$mytitle`) and some text (`$mytext`)
- Lastly, we want the controller to accept a parameter from the user (i.e. via the URL request)

In other words, we have to populate the variables in the view. So let's start with our `Start` controller. This is an OO class:

```php
<?php
class Start extends Controller {
    var     $base;
    var     $css;
```

Notice that here we've declared the `$base` (the web root address), and `$css` (the css filename) as variables or class properties. This saves us from having to re-declare them if we write more than one function in each class. But you can define and use them as local variables within one function, if you prefer.

The constructor function now defines the properties we've declared, by looking them up in the `config` file. To do this, we use the syntax:

```
$this->config->item('name_of_config_variable');
```

as in:

```
function Start()
{
        parent::Controller();
        $this->base = $this->config->item('base_url');
        $this->css = $this->config->item('css');
}
```

and CI recovers whatever we entered in the `config` file against that name.

Using this system, however many controllers and functions we write, we'll only have to change these fundamental variables once, even if our site becomes so popular that we have to move it to a bigger server.

Getting Parameters to a Function

Now, within the `Start` controller class, let's define the function that will actually do the work.

```
function hello($name)
{
  $data['css'] = $this->css;
  $data['base'] = $this->base;
  $data['mytitle'] = 'Welcome to this site';
  $data['mytext'] = "Hello, $name, now we're getting dynamic!";
  $this->load->view('testview', $data);
}
```

This function expects a parameter, `$name`, (but you can set a default value— `myfunction($myvariable = 0)`), which it uses to build up the string assigned to the `$mytext` variable. Well, as we had just asked, where does that come from?

In this case, it needs to come from the URL request, where it will be the third parameter. So, it comes via the HTTP request:

```
GET /index.php/start/hello/fred HTTP/1.0
```

Or in other words, when you type in the URL:

```
http://www.mysite.com/index.php/start/hello/fred
```

 Note that this example code doesn't 'clean' the passed variable `fred`, or check it in any way. You might want to do this in production code. We'll look at how to check form inputs in Chapter 7. Normally, variables passed by hyperlinks in this way are generated by your own site. A malicious user could easily add his or her own, just by sending a URL like: `http://www.mysite.com/index.php/start/hello/my_malicious_variable`. So, you might want to check that the variables you receive are within the range you expect before handling them.

The last segment of the URL is passed to the function as a parameter. In fact, you can add more segments of extra parameters if you like, subject to the practical limits imposed by your browser.

Let's recap on how CI handles URLs, since we've covered it all now:

URL segment	What it Does
`http://www.mysite.com`	The base URL that finds your site.
`/index.php`	Finds the CI router that sets about reading the rest of the URL and selecting the correct route into your site.
`/start`	The name of the controller CI will call. (If no name is set, CI will call whichever default controller you've specified.)
`/hello`	The name of a function that CI will call, inside the selected controller. (If no function is specified, defaults to the index function, unless you've used `_remap`.)
`/fred`	CI passes this to the function as a variable.
If there is a further URL segment, e.g. `/bert`	CI passes this to the function as a second variable.
More variables	*CI will pass further URL segments on as further variables.*

Passing Data to a View

Let's go back to the hello function:

```
function hello($name)
{
  $data['css'] = $this->css;
  $data['base'] = $this->base;
  $data['mytitle'] = 'Welcome to this site';
  $data['mytext'] = "Hello, $name, now we're getting dynamic!";
  $this->load->view('testview', $data);
}
```

Notice how the `hello()` function first creates an array called $data, taking a mixture of object properties set up by the constructor and text.

Then it loads the view by name, with the array it has just built as the second parameter.

Behind the scenes, CI makes good use of another PHP function: `extract()`. This takes each value in the $data array and turns it into a new variable in its own right—so the $data array that we've just defined is received by the view as a series of separate variables: $text (equal to `"Hello, $name, now we're getting dynamic"`), $css (equal to the value from the `config` file), and so on.

In other words, when it is built, the $data array looks like this:

```
Array
(
  [css] => mystyles.css
  [base] => http://127.0.0.1/packt
  [mytitle] => Welcome to this site
  [mytext] => Hello, fred, now we're getting dynamic!
)
```

But on the way to the view, it is unpacked, and the following variables are created in the view to correspond to each key/value pair in the array:

```
$css     = 'mystyles.css';
$base    = 'http://127.0.0.1/packt';
$mytitle = 'Welcome to this site';
$mytext  = 'Hello, fred, now we're getting dynamic!';
)
```

Although you can only pass one variable to a view, you can pack a lot of information into that one variable. Each value in the $data array can itself be another array, and so on, so you can pass pieces of information to the view in a tightly structured manner.

Now navigate to `http://127.0.0.1/packt/index.php/index/start/fred` (note that the URL is different—it is looking for the `start` function we wrote in the `index` controller) and you'll see the result: a dynamic page written using MVC architecture. (Well, VC at least! We haven't really used the M yet.)

Here's what it should look like now:

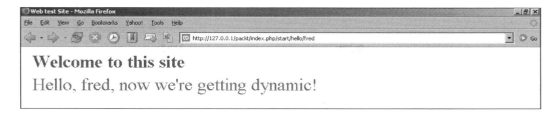

You can see (at least I hope you can!) that the parameter `fred` is the last segment of the URL. It has been passed into the function, and then through to the view.

Please remember that your view must be written in parallel with your controller. If the view does not expect and make a place for a variable, it won't be displayed. If the view is expecting a variable to be set and it isn't, you are likely to get an error message. (Your view can of course accept variables conditionally.)

How CI Classes Pass Information and Control to Each Other

As you write your controllers, models, etc., you will need to pass control and data between them. Let's look at some of the ways in which we can do this.

Calling Views

We have seen how the controller calls a view and passes data to it:

First it creates an array of data ($data) to pass to the view; then it loads and calls the view in the same expression:

```
$this->load->view('testview', $data);
```

Calling Functions Directly

If you want to use code from libraries, models, plug-ins, or helpers, of course, you have to load them first, and then call them as described in the previous table. So, if 'display' is a model and I want to use its `mainpage` function, my controller might call:

```
$this->display->mainpage();
```

If the function requires parameters, we can pass them to the function like this:

```
$this->display->mainpage('parameter1', $parameter2);
```

Interacting with Controllers

You can call libraries, models, plug-ins, or helpers from within any controller, and models and libraries can also call each other as well as plug-ins and helpers.

However, you can't call one controller from another, or call a controller from a model or library. There are only two ways that a model or a library can refer back to a controller:

Firstly, it can return data. If the controller assigns a value like this:

```
$fred = $this->mymodel->myfunction();
```

and the function is set to return a value, then that value will be passed to the variable $fred inside the controller.

Secondly, your model or library can create (and send to a view) a URL, which allows a human user to call the controller functions. Controllers are there to receive human interactions.

You can't, of course, hyperlink directly to a model or library. Users always talk to controllers, never to anything else—but you can write a calling function in the controller. In other words, your view might contain a hyperlink to a controller function:

```
echo anchor(start/callmodel, Do something with a model);
```

but the `callmodel` function would exit only to call a function in the model:

```
function callmodel()

{
  $this->load->model(mymodel);
  $this->mymodel->myfunction();
}
```

It's Just Like an Egg-Cup

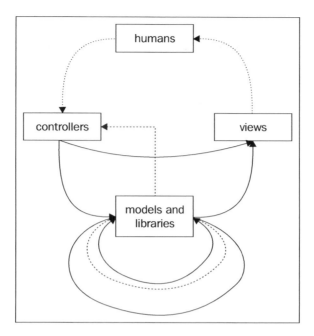

This diagram shows the different ways in which components can address each other.

Unbroken lines represent direct function calls such as:

```
$this->mymodel->myfunction();
```

These can take place from controllers to views, and from controllers to libraries or models. (Models can also call views, but probably shouldn't.) They can't take place in reverse: views etc. can't call controllers. However, libraries and models can call each other and be called by each other.

Broken lines represent passing information by returning values. Models and libraries can do this to controllers, or to each other. Views don't return values.

The dotted lines represent passing information or control via a human user—in other words, the view will show the user something on the screen and may invite the user to click on a hyperlink (which sets off a controller).

Any resemblance to an egg-cup is purely coincidental. It just came out that way.

An Example of a CI Helper: the URL Helper

As an example of the way you can split your code up into neat, focussed, chunks, CI's URL helper contains a set of functions that help you to manipulate URLs. You load it like this:

```
this->load->helper('url');
```

And then, you can use it to find and return the site and/or base URLs that you set in your `config` file:

```
echo site_url();
echo base_url();
```

You can also use it to create hyperlinks. We saw in the last section how you can access the `hello` function in the `start` controller, and pass it the parameter `fred`, with a URL like:

http://www.mysite.com/index.php/start/hello/fred

If you want your own code to create a hyperlink to a URL like this, you can use the URL helper to do it. The syntax is:

```
echo anchor(start/hello/fred, Say hello to Fred);
```

This generates a hyperlink to the same URL, and displays the words `Say hello to Fred` to the user to be clicked on. In other words, it's the equivalent of:

```
<a href="http://www.mysite.com/index.php/start/hello/fred ">say hello
to Fred</a>
```

Remember, there are two advantages to using the CI helper. Firstly, less typing (49 characters as opposed to 82, both including spaces. If you include loading the URL helper—another 27 characters, which you only have to do once per controller—it still comes to 76 rather than 82.)

Secondly, the URL helper automatically looks up the site URL in the `config` files (and the index file name). This means that if you change your site location, you only need to alter the `config` file once, you don't have to hunt through your code for hyperlinks that don't work any more.

The URL helper has other useful functions. For instance, it can create a 'mailto' hyperlink.

```
echo mailto('me@example.com', 'Click Here to Email Me');
```

has the same effect as typing this HTML:

```
<a href="mailto:me@example.com">click here to email me</a>
```

If you are worried about robots harvesting the email addresses from your website and using them for spamming, change `mailto` in the CI code to `safe_mailto`. What appears on your viewer's screen is exactly the same, and works the same way.

However, if you examine the actual HTML code, this has now become a complex heap of JavaScript, which the robot cannot (easily) read:

```
<script type="text/javascript">
//<![CDATA[
var l=new Array();
l[0]='>';l[1]='a';l[2]='/
';l[3]='<';l[4]='|101';l[5]='|109';l[6]='|32';l[7]='|108';l[8]='|105'
;l[9]='|97';l[10]='|109';l[11]='|101';l[12]='|32';l[13]='|111';l[14]=
'|116';l[15]='|32';l[16]='|101';l[17]='|114';l[18]='|101';l[19]='|72'
;l[20]='|32';l[21]='|107';l[22]='|99';l[23]='|105';l[24]='|108';l[25]
='|67';l[26]='>';l[27]='"';l[28]='|109';l[29]='|111';l[30]='|99';l[31
]='|46';l[32]='|101';l[33]='|108';l[34]='|112';l[35]='|109';l[36]='|9
7';l[37]='|120';l[38]='|101';l[39]='|64';l[40]='|101';l[41]='|109';l
[42]=':';l[43]='o';l[44]='t';l[45]='l';l[46]='i';l[47]='a';l[48]='m'
;l[49]='"';l[50]='=';l[51]='f';l[52]='e';l[53]='r';l[54]='h';l[55]='
';l[56]='a';l[57]='<';
for (var i = l.length-1; i >= 0; i=i-1){
if (l[i].substring(0, 1) == '|') document.write("&#"+unescape(l[i].
substring(1))+";");
else document.write(unescape(l[i]));}
//]]>
</script>
```

You, and your users, need never see this code. It's only there to confuse the robots and keep your email addresses safe from spam. You put it there by adding four letters and an underscore: you wrote `safe_mailto` instead of `mailto`, and CI did the rest.

There are several other useful functions in the URL helper. See the User Guide for more about them and how to use them.

Just consider the URL helper as a whole. Let's go back to the touchstones for coding we discussed earlier in this chapter:

- This code has high 'component singularity'. It does a limited range of things, and it's clear what they are.

- It is 'loosely coupled' — it has a simple interface and no other dependency on any code that's calling it. You can use the URL helper in any CI project you're writing. Most of your projects will need some sort of hyperlinks, for instance. You can use this helper over and over again to create them.

If you look at the URL helper's code (in `system/application/helpers/url_helper.php`) you'll see that it is procedural code—that is, it is simply a set of functions, not an OO class. It doesn't load any other CI classes or helpers. (Not being an object, it can't do this.)

A Simple Library Example: Creating a Menu

Now let's look at some code that does use the CI classes.

For instance, here is a simple library file that creates a menu with three choices:

```php
1  <?php
2  class Menu{
3  function show_menu()
4    {
5    $obj =& get_instance();
6    $obj->load->helper('url');
7    $menu  = anchor("start/hello/fred","Say hello to Fred |");
8    $menu  .= anchor("start/hello/bert","Say hello to Bert |");
9    $menu  .= anchor("start/another_function","Do something else |");
10   return $menu;
11   }
12  }
13  ?>
```

(For the moment, don't worry about the unusual syntax—`$obj->` rather than `$this->` in line 6. This is exaplained in Chapter 7.)

Note that this code is now OO code, in which the function `show_menu()` is contained in a single class, 'Menu'. It can access other CI classes and helpers: in this case it is using the URL helper, which we just examined.

Firstly, it loads the URL helper, and then it creates a string (`$menu`), consisting of HTML code for hyperlinks to the three controllers and functions specified to it. Then it returns the `$menu` string.

You might call it from a controller like this:

```php
$mymenu  = $this->menu->show_menu();
```

and then the controller can use the `$menu` variable to call a view:

```php
$data['menu'] = $mymenu;
$this->load->view('myview', $data);
```

This class produces a menu, which is site-specific. For this reason, I would save it in the `/system/application/libraries`, rather than the `system/libraries`, folder. It's not as loosely coupled as the URL helper, which I can use on any site.

It does have high singularity: it creates a menu, and that's all it does. I can call it from any controller in my site and know that it will show the standard menu in my models.

Summary

The MVC framework is a widely used and very effective way of organizing a complex website. CI uses it to help you sort out your own code, but it is also fairly flexible about how it does so.

Try to keep in mind the two principles of 'loose coupling' and 'component singularity' when you write your own code. Don't worry too much whether your application conforms to the strict theory of MVC or not. The crucial thing is to understand what the different types of file are, and how they relate to each other. Then, you can decide whether to write your own code in library or model files, or as helpers or plug-ins.

We've looked at the CI file structure, and seen how you can, if you want, inspect all the CI code, but (thankfully!) you don't have to.

We did tinker with one of the original files: the `config` file, which holds critical site information in one place to make it easier for us to upgrade or change later on.

We've seen the basic object structure of a controller, and used a simple constructor to get some data from our `config` file and put it into a class property. And we've dynamically passed information from a new controller we wrote, to a new view. So far, the main thing CI has done for us is to encourage us to use a basic structure as we start to define our site. As we go on, it will become clear just how important that structure is.

Also, we looked a the way that CI's components pass data and control between themselves. It's useful to understand this when you start to write your code.

Lastly, we looked at CI's own URL helper as a good example of a chunk of code, and we wrote our own rudimentary 'menu' library class.

4
Using CI to Simplify Databases

You're looking at CI because you want to make coding easier and more productive. This chapter is about CI's **Active Record** class. If CI offered nothing more than its Active Record class, it would still be worth every penny of the purchase price. All right, it's free. I'll rephrase that—it would still be a major tool to increase your productivity.

Active Record allows you to handle databases with a minimum of fuss and a maximum of clarity. It's simple to use and maintain.

This chapter looks at how you set up a database to work with CI, and then how you use the Active Record class to manipulate the database. You'll see:

- How Active Record code compares with 'classic' PHP/ MySQL interface code
- How to write 'read' queries, and display the results
- How to do create, update, and delete queries

CI allows you to write queries in the traditional 'classic' PHP style as well, but I won't go into detail on that. It's fully covered in the online User Guide. I started off doing it the old way, but once I tried Active Record, I never looked back.

Configuration Settings

You have probably noticed that most chapters in this book keep going back to the `system/application/config` folder and the configuration files inside it. These are pretty essential for controlling the way CI works. And while you can leave most of them safely set at the defaults, the `database` config file does need tweaking before anything will work at all.

Basically, you just have to tell it where your database is, and what type it is. The default file simply says:

```
$active_group = "default";
$db['default']['hostname'] = "";
$db['default']['username'] = "";
$db['default']['password'] = "";
$db['default']['database'] = "";
$db['default']['dbdriver'] = "";
```

along with a few other options that you can leave at the default, for now. The options you must fill in are:

- `hostname`: The location of your database, e.g., 'localhost' or an IP address
- `username` and `password`: The username and password of a database user with sufficient permissions to do whatever you may want your site to do. This is not (usually) the same username and password as your site or your ISP's control panel.
- `database`: The name of your database, e.g., 'websites'
- `dbdriver`: The type of database you're using—at the time of writing, the options CI offers were MySQL, MySQLi, Postgre SQL, ODBC, and MS SQL.

In my experience, one of the most difficult things to set up on a new CI site can be the link to the database. You may need to consult your ISP if in doubt—sometimes their database runs at a different address to their web servers. If you are using MySQL, they may offer phpMyAdmin, which usually tells you the hostname—this may be 'localhost' or it may be an IP address.

You'll note that this part of the `config` file is actually a multi-dimensional array. Within `$db` is an array called `default`, and you're adding key/variable pairs like `hostname = 127.0.0.1` to that array. This is so that you can set up other databases, as other secondary arrays, and swap between them easily by simply changing the `$active_group` setting to the name of another array.

This makes it possible to run a site with several database options—for instance, a test database and a production database—and to swap between them easily. Or you might need to draw information from two separate databases.

Designing the Database for Our Site

I want to show that CI can be used to develop a serious website with a serious purpose. I am currently running several websites for clients, and I want a program that will monitor them, test them in ways I specify, keep a database of what it has done, and let me have reports when I want them. So let's try to build it. Firstly let's set some objectives. These are:

1. To manage one or more remote websites with a minimum of human intervention

2. To run regular tests on the remote sites

3. To generate reports on demand, giving details of the site and of tests conducted

So, the first thing we will need is a database of websites to check. Set up a database called `websites` in MySQL or whatever RDBMS you're using.

Now, we need to add some tables to hold various types of data. Let's add to our `websites` database a table for sites, which includes fields for their URLs, their names and password/usernames, and their types. We'll also include an `id` field for each site—and in MySQL at least, which can be set to generate a unique new ID for each entry, using the auto-increment field type.

Each site may be hosted with a different host, or host machine, and we need another `hosts` table to store data about this. It most probably has a domain associated with it, so we need a `domains` table to keep track of data about the domain, like when it's due for renewal, the registrar, and our username/password on the registrar site. Then of course, we have those tiresome people, clients, some of whom may own more than one site, so we need a separate `people` table in which to store their names, email addresses, snail mail addresses, mobile numbers, plus pet's names, and all the other stuff so vital to good CRM.

So our site table needs to include fields for a domain ID, a host ID, and perhaps a couple of people IDs, one for the site owner or client and one for the site manager. (That's you, or one of the staff you'll have to hire to keep pace when this app hits the market.)

As you can see, this is a full relational database, and we've only just started! (Fuller details of this database are set out as an appendix to this chapter, in the form of a MySQL query, if you want to set one up yourself.)

We're going to want a simple flexible way of accessing all this. So, let's turn to what CI can offer, and in particular to its Active Record class.

Active Record

'Active Record' is a 'design pattern'—another of those highly abstract systems like MVC, which provide templates for solving common coding problems and also generate some of the dullest books on the planet. In itself, it isn't code, just a pattern for code. There are several different interpretations of it. At its core is the creation of a relationship between your database and an object, every time you do a query. Typically, each table is a class, and each single row becomes an object. All the things you might want to do with a table row—create it, read it, update it, or delete it, for example—become 'methods', which that object inherits from its class. Ruby on Rails is built around the Active Record pattern, and so is CI—although the exact implementation in the two frameworks seems to have subtle differences.

Enough theory—what does it mean? Well, simple and clear code statements, if you don't mind putting arrows in them.

Advantages of Using the Active Record Class

Active record saves you time, brings in automatic functionality that you don't have to think about, and makes SQL statements easy to understand.

Saving Time

When you write a normal database query in PHP, you must write a connection to the database each time. With CI, you connect once to the database, by putting the following line in the constructor function of each controller or model:

```
$this->load->database();
```

Once you've done this, you don't have to repeat the connection, how many ever queries you then make in that controller or model.

You set up the database details in the config files as we saw earlier in this chapter. Once again, this makes it easier to update your site, if you ever change the database name, password, or location.

Automatic Functionality

Once you've connected to the database, CI's active record syntax brings hidden code with it. For instance, if you enter the following 'insert' query:

```
$data = array(
            'title' => $title,
            'name' => $name,
            'date' => $date
        );
$this->db->insert('mytable', $data);
```

the values you are inserting have been escaped behind the scenes by this code:

```
function escape($str)
{
```

```
    switch (gettype($str))
    {case 'string':
    $str = "'".$this->escape_str($str)."'";
    break;
    case 'boolean':      $str = ($str === FALSE) ? 0 : 1;
    break;
    default       :       $str = ($str === NULL) ? 'NULL' : $str;
    break;
    }
return $str;
}
```

In other words, the CI framework is making your code more robust. Now, let's look at how it works.

Firstly, connecting to the database is very simple. In classic PHP, you might say something like this:

```
$connection = mysql_connect("localhost","fred","12345");
mysql_select_db("websites", $connection);
$result = mysql_query ("SELECT * FROM sites", $connection);
while ($row = mysql_fetch_array($result, MYSQL_NUM))
{
   foreach ($row as $attribute)
      print "{$attribute[1]} ";
}
```

In other words, you have to re-state the host, username, and password, make a connection, then select the database from that connection. You have to do this each time. Only then, do you get on to the actual query. CI replaces the connection stuff with one line:

```
$this->load->database();
```

which you put once, in each controller or model or class constructor that you write. After that, in each function within those controllers, etc., you just go straight into your query. The connection information is stored in your database config file, and CI goes and looks it up there each time.

So, in each CI function, you go straight to your query. The query above written in CI comes out as:

```
$query = $this->db->get('sites');
   foreach ($query->result() as $row)
   {
      print $row->url
   }
```

Simple, isn't it?

The rest of this chapter sets out ways of making different queries, making them more specific.

Read Queries

The most common query that we'll write simply retrieves information from the database according to our criteria. The basic instruction to perform a read query is:

```
$query = $this->db->get('sites');
```

This is a 'SELECT *' query on the `sites` table—in other words, it retrieves all the fields. If you prefer to specify the target table (`sites`) in a separate line, you can do so in this way:

```
$this->db->from('sites');
$query = $this->db->get();
```

If you want to 'SELECT' or limit the number of fields retrieved, rather than get them all, use this instruction:

```
$this->db->select('url','name','clientid');
$query = $this->db->get('sites');
```

You may want to present the results in a particular order—say by the site name—in which case you insert (before the `$this->db->get` line):

```
$this->db->orderby("name", "desc");
```

`desc` means in descending order. You can also choose `asc` (ascending) or `rand` (random).

You may also want to limit the number of results your query displays; say you want only the first five results. In this case insert:

```
$this->db->limit(5);
```

Of course, in most queries, you're not likely to ask for every record in the table. The power of databases depends on their ability to select—to pick out the one piece of data you want from the piles of stuff you don't. This is usually done by a `where` statement that CI expresses in this way:

```
$this->db->where('clientid', '1');
```

This statement would find all websites linked to the client whose ID was 1. But that's not much help to us. We don't want to remember all the ID's in our `people` table. As humans, we prefer to remember human names. So we need to link in the `people` table:

```
$this->db->from('sites');
$this->db->join('people', 'sites.peopleid = people.id');
```

For each people ID in the `sites` table, look up the information against that ID in the `people` table as well.

 Note the SQL convention that if a field name may be ambiguous between two tables, you reference it with the table name first, then a period, then the field name. So `sites.peopleid` means the `peopleid` field in the `sites` table. In fact, there isn't a field called `peopleid` in both tables, but there is an `id` field in both `sites` and `people`, so the RDBMS will protest if you try to run the query without resolving the ambiguity for it. In any case, it's a good habit to make your meaning explicit, and CI syntax happily accepts the fuller names.

You can play around with the syntax of `where` statements. For instance, add negation operators:

```
$this->db->where('url !=','www.mysite.com' );
```

or comparison operators:

```
$this->db->where('id >','3' );
```

or combine statements ("WHERE... AND..."):

```
$this->db->where('url !=','www.mysite.com');
$this->db->where('id >', '3');
```

or use `$this->db->orwhere()` to search for alternatives ("WHERE ... OR"):

```
$this->db->where('url !=','www.mysite.com' );
$this->db->orwhere('url !=','www.anothersite.com' );
```

So let's say we've built up a query like this:

```
$this->db->select('url','name','clientid','people.surname AS client');
$this->db->where('clientid', '3');
$this->db->limit(5);
$this->db->from('sites');
$this->db->join('people', 'sites.clientid = people.id');
$this->db->orderby("name", "desc");
$query = $this->db->get();
```

This should give us the first five (ordered by name) websites belonging to client number 3, and fetch the client's surname as well as his or her ID number!

A hidden benefit of using Active Record is that data that may have come in from users is automatically escaped, so you don't have to worry about putting quotes around it. This applies to functions like `$this->db->where()`, and also to the data creation and update statements described in the next sections. (Security warning: this is not the same thing as preventing cross-scripting attacks—for that you need CI's `xss_clean()` function. It's also not the same as validating your data—for this you need CI's validation class. See Chapter 5.)

Displaying Query Results

Showing database query results in CI is quite simple. We define our query as above, ending in:

```
$query = $this->db->get();
```

Then, if there are multiple results, they can be returned as a `$row` object through which you iterate with a `foreach` loop:

```
foreach ($query->result() as $row)
{
    print $row->url;
    print $row->name;
    print $row->client;
}
```

or if we only want a single result, it can be returned as an object, or here as a `$row` array:

```
if ($query->num_rows() > 0)
{
    $row = $query->row_array();

    print $row['url'];
    print $row['name'];
    print $row['client'];
}
```

Personally, I prefer the object syntax to the array—less typing!

When you follow the MVC pattern, you will usually want to keep your queries and database interactions in models, and display the information through views.

Create and Update Queries

Active Record has three functions that help you create new entries in your database. They are `$this->db->insert()`, `$this->db->update()`, and `$this->db->set()`.

The difference between a 'create' and an 'update' query is that when you create a new record, there is no reference to any existing record, you are writing a new one. When you update, there is an existing record, and you are changing it. So in the second case, you have to specify which record you are changing. In both cases, you have to set the values you want to leave in the database after your query. Values you don't set will be left unaltered—or, if they didn't exist before, they will still be 'null' after your query.

CI allows you to set your values either with an array, or with `$this->db-set()`; the difference is only one of syntax.

So, let's add a line to our `sites` table in the `websites` database. We've already connected to this database in our controller. The controller's constructor function included the line:

```
$this->load->database();
```

We want to add a new site, which has a URL, a name, a type, and a client ID number. As an array, this might be:

```
$data = array(
            'url' => 'www.mynewclient.com',
            'name' => 'BigCo Inc',
            'clientid' => '33',
            'type' => 'dynamic'
        );
```

To add that to the `sites` table, we follow it with:

```
$this->db->insert('sites', $data);
```

Alternatively, we could set each value using `$this->db->set()`:

```
$this->db->set('url', 'www.mynewclinet.com');
$this->db->set('name', 'BigCo Inc');
$this->db->set('clientid', '33');
$this->db->set('type', 'dynamic');
$this->db->insert('sites');
```

If we are updating an existing record, then again we can either create an array, or use `$this->db->set()`. But there are two differences.

Firstly, we have to specify the record we want to update; and second, we need to use `$this->db->update()`. If I want to update a record (say the record with its 'id' field set to 1) in my `sites` table, using the data set out in my `$data` array above, the syntax is:

```
$this->db->where('id', '1');
$this->db->update('sites', $data);
```

Or I can set out the information using `$this->db->set()`, as above.

CI gives you several functions to check what the database has done. Most usefully:

```
$this->db->affected_rows();
```

should return '1' after my insert or update statement—but might show more rows if I was altering several rows of data at one time. You can use it to check that the operation has done what you expected.

You've noticed that I didn't set an ID field when I created a new record. That's because we set the database to populate the ID field automatically when a new record is added. But I do have to specify an ID when I update an existing record, otherwise the database doesn't know which one to alter.

If I'm generating a new record, however, I don't know the ID number until I've generated it. If I then need to refer to the new record, I can get the new ID number with:

```
$new_id_number = $this->db->insert_id();
```

(This code has to go, as soon as possible, after the operation that generated the record, or it may give a misleading result.)

For a little more peace of mind, remember that CI Active Record functions, including `$this->db->insert()` and `$this->db->update()` automatically escape data passed to them as input.

From version 1.5, CI also includes support for transactions—linking two or more database actions together so that they either all succeed, or all fail. This is essential in double-entry book-keeping applications and many commercial sites. For instance, say you are selling theatre tickets. You record receiving a payment in one transaction, and then allocate a seat to the customer in another. If your system fails after doing the first database operation, but before doing the second, you may end up with an angry customer—who has been charged, but has not had a seat reserved.

CI now makes it much simpler to link two or more database operations into one transaction, so that if they all succeed, the transaction is 'committed', and if one or more fails, the transaction is 'rolled back'. We don't need to use this in our example site, but if you want more information see the CI online User Guide.

Delete Queries

Delete queries are perhaps the simplest to describe. All you need is the name of the table and the ID number of the record to delete. Let's say I want to delete record in my `sites` table with the ID number 2:

```
$this->db->where('id', '2');
$this->db->delete('sites');
```

I get slightly nervous around 'delete' queries because they are so powerful. Please remember to make sure that there is a valid value in the 'where' clause, or you may delete your whole table! Neither the author nor Packt Publishing will accept any liability if….

Mixing Active Record and 'Classic' Styles

CI doesn't insist that you use Active Record. You can also use CI to issue straight SQL queries. For instance, assuming you loaded the database in your constructor, you can still write queries like this:

```
$this->db->query("SELECT id, name, url FROM sites WHERE 'type' =
'dynamic'");
```

Personally, I find Active Record easier to use. Conceptually, setting out my query in an array makes it easier to see and manipulate as an entity than writing it in SQL syntax. It's slightly more verbose, but clearly structured; it automatically escapes data; and it may be more portable. It also minimizes typing errors with commas and quotes.

There are a few cases, however, where you may have to resort to the original SQL. You might want to do complex joins, or another example is if you need to use multiple 'where' conditions. If you want to find the websites associated with client 3, but only those of two specific types, you may need to put brackets around the SQL to make sure the query is correctly interpreted.

In cases like these, you can always write out the SQL as a string, put it in a variable, and use the variable in CI's `$this->db->where()` function, as follows:

```
$condition = "client ='3' AND (type ='dynamic' OR type='static')";
$this->db->where($condition); .
```

Without the brackets this is ambiguous. Do you mean:

```
(client='3' AND type = 'dynamic') OR type = 'static'
```

or

```
client='3' AND (type = 'dynamic' OR type = 'static')
```

Well, yes of course, it's obvious, but the machine usually guesses wrong. Incidentally, be careful with the syntax of `$condition`. The actual SQL query is:

```
client='3' AND (type = 'dynamic' OR type = 'static')
```

The double quotes come from the variable assignment:

```
$condition = "    ";
```

It's easy to get your single and double quotes confused.

Some of the CI expressions I've quoted above, like `$this->db->affected_rows()`, are not a part of its Active Record model. But they can be mixed in easily.

The only time you might run into problems is if you try to mix Active Record and straight SQL in the same query. (I haven't tried this. If you have a lot of time on your hands, you could test it out, but frankly, I think that would indicate a sad lifestyle. Try train-spotting instead. At least it gets you out into the fresh air! I use CI because I'm too busy not to!)

Summary

We've looked at CI's Active Record class and seen how easy it is to:

- Set up connections to one or more databases
- Do standard SQL read, update, create, and delete queries
- Perform other functions that we need, to use a database properly

CI's Active Record function is clean and easy to use, and makes coding much clearer to read. It automates database connections, allowing you to abstract the connection information to one config file.

It can do pretty well anything that you can do with 'classic' SQL—more than I have space to explain here. See the online User Guide for fuller details.

Chapter Appendix: MYSQL Query to Set Up 'websites' Database

```
DROP TABLE IF EXISTS `ci_sessions`;
CREATE TABLE IF NOT EXISTS `ci_sessions` (
  `session_id` varchar(40) NOT NULL default '0',
  `peopleid` int(11) NOT NULL,
  `ip_address` varchar(16) NOT NULL default '0',
  `user_agent` varchar(50) NOT NULL,
  `last_activity` int(10) unsigned NOT NULL default '0',
  `left` int(11) NOT NULL,
  `name` varchar(25) NOT NULL,
  `status` tinyint(4) NOT NULL default '0'
) ENGINE=MyISAM DEFAULT CHARSET=latin1;

DROP TABLE IF EXISTS `domains`;
CREATE TABLE IF NOT EXISTS `domains` (
  `id` int(10) NOT NULL auto_increment,
  `url` varchar(100) NOT NULL,
  `name` varchar(100) NOT NULL,
  `registrar` varchar(100) NOT NULL,
  `dateregd` int(11) NOT NULL default '0',
  `cost` float NOT NULL default '0',
  `regdfor` int(11) NOT NULL default '0',
  `notes` blob NOT NULL,
  `pw` varchar(25) NOT NULL,
  `un` varchar(25) NOT NULL,
  `lastupdate` int(11) NOT NULL default '0',
  `submit` varchar(25) NOT NULL,
  PRIMARY KEY  (`id`)
) ENGINE=MyISAM DEFAULT CHARSET=latin1 AUTO_INCREMENT=10 ;

DROP TABLE IF EXISTS `events`;
CREATE TABLE IF NOT EXISTS `events` (
  `id` int(10) NOT NULL auto_increment,
  `name` varchar(50) NOT NULL default 'not set',
  `type` enum('test','alert','report') NOT NULL,
  `testid` int(10) NOT NULL,
  `siteid` int(10) NOT NULL,
  `userid` int(10) NOT NULL,
  `reported` int(11) NOT NULL,
  `result` blob NOT NULL,
  `time` int(11) NOT NULL,
```

```
   `timetaken` float NOT NULL,
   `isalert` varchar(2) NOT NULL,
   `emailid` int(11) NOT NULL,
   `submit` varchar(25) NOT NULL,
   PRIMARY KEY  (`id`)
) ENGINE=MyISAM DEFAULT CHARSET=latin1 AUTO_INCREMENT=69 ;

DROP TABLE IF EXISTS `frequencies`;
CREATE TABLE IF NOT EXISTS `frequencies` (
   `id` int(10) NOT NULL,
   `name` varchar(16) NOT NULL,
   `submit` varchar(25) NOT NULL,
   PRIMARY KEY  (`id`)
) ENGINE=MyISAM DEFAULT CHARSET=latin1;

DROP TABLE IF EXISTS `hosts`;
CREATE TABLE IF NOT EXISTS `hosts` (
   `id` int(11) NOT NULL auto_increment,
   `cost` float NOT NULL,
   `name` varchar(100) NOT NULL,
   `hosturl` varchar(100) NOT NULL,
   `un` varchar(50) NOT NULL,
   `pw` varchar(50) NOT NULL,
   `ns1url` varchar(36) NOT NULL,
   `ns1ip` varchar(36) NOT NULL,
   `ns2url` varchar(36) NOT NULL,
   `ns2ip` varchar(36) NOT NULL,
   `ftpurl` varchar(100) NOT NULL,
   `ftpserverip` varchar(36) NOT NULL,
   `ftpun` varchar(50) NOT NULL,
   `ftppw` varchar(50) NOT NULL,
   `cpurl` varchar(36) NOT NULL,
   `cpun` varchar(36) NOT NULL,
   `cppw` varchar(36) NOT NULL,
   `pop3server` varchar(36) NOT NULL,
   `servicetel` varchar(50) NOT NULL,
   `servicetel2` varchar(50) NOT NULL,
   `serviceemail` varchar(100) NOT NULL,
   `webroot` varchar(48) NOT NULL,
   `absoluteroot` varchar(48) NOT NULL,
   `cgiroot` varchar(48) NOT NULL,
   `booked` int(11) NOT NULL,
   `duration` int(11) NOT NULL,
   `lastupdate` int(11) NOT NULL default '0',
```

```
    `submit` varchar(25) NOT NULL,
    PRIMARY KEY  (`id`)
) ENGINE=MyISAM DEFAULT CHARSET=latin1 AUTO_INCREMENT=6 ;

DROP TABLE IF EXISTS `people`;
CREATE TABLE IF NOT EXISTS `people` (
    `id` int(11) NOT NULL auto_increment,
    `uname` varchar(25) NOT NULL,
    `pw` varchar(25) NOT NULL,
    `status` smallint(3) NOT NULL default '1',
    `name` varchar(50) NOT NULL,
    `firstname` varchar(50) NOT NULL,
    `surname` varchar(50) NOT NULL,
    `email` varchar(120) NOT NULL,
    `lastupdate` int(11) NOT NULL default '0',
    `submit` varchar(25) NOT NULL,
    PRIMARY KEY  (`id`)
) ENGINE=MyISAM DEFAULT CHARSET=latin1 AUTO_INCREMENT=5 ;

DROP TABLE IF EXISTS `sites`;
CREATE TABLE IF NOT EXISTS `sites` (
    `id` int(10) NOT NULL auto_increment,
    `name` varchar(100) NOT NULL,
    `url` varchar(100) NOT NULL,
    `un` varchar(50) NOT NULL,
    `pw` varchar(50) NOT NULL,
    `client1` int(10) NOT NULL default '0',
    `client2` int(10) NOT NULL default '0',
    `admin1` int(10) NOT NULL default '0',
    `admin2` int(10) NOT NULL default '0',
    `domainid` int(10) NOT NULL default '0',
    `hostid` int(10) NOT NULL default '0',
    `webroot` varchar(50) NOT NULL,
    `files` text NOT NULL,
    `filesdate` int(11) NOT NULL default '0',
    `lastupdate` int(11) NOT NULL default '0',
    `submit` varchar(25) NOT NULL,
    PRIMARY KEY  (`id`)
) ENGINE=MyISAM DEFAULT CHARSET=latin1 AUTO_INCREMENT=15 ;

DROP TABLE IF EXISTS `tests`;
CREATE TABLE IF NOT EXISTS `tests` (
    `id` int(11) NOT NULL auto_increment,
    `siteid` int(11) NOT NULL default '0',
```

```
  `name` varchar(250) NOT NULL,
  `type` varchar(25) NOT NULL,
  `url` varchar(120) NOT NULL,
  `regex` varchar(250) NOT NULL,
  `p1` varchar(250) NOT NULL,
  `p2` varchar(250) NOT NULL,
  `p3` varchar(250) NOT NULL,
  `p4` varchar(250) NOT NULL,
  `p5` varchar(250) NOT NULL,
  `p6` varchar(250) NOT NULL,
  `frequency` int(10) NOT NULL default '0',
  `lastdone` int(10) NOT NULL default '0',
  `isalert` varchar(2) NOT NULL,
  `setup` int(10) NOT NULL default '0',
  `lastupdate` int(10) NOT NULL default '0',
  `notes` varchar(250) NOT NULL,
  `submit` varchar(25) NOT NULL,
  PRIMARY KEY  (`id`)
) ENGINE=MyISAM DEFAULT CHARSET=latin1 AUTO_INCREMENT=11 ;

DROP TABLE IF EXISTS `types`;
CREATE TABLE IF NOT EXISTS `types` (
  `id` varchar(7) NOT NULL,
  `name` varchar(50) NOT NULL,
  PRIMARY KEY  (`id`)
) ENGINE=MyISAM DEFAULT CHARSET=latin1;
```

5
Simplifying HTML Pages and Forms

This chapter covers yet another way in which CI helps save your time and make your coding more rigorous and logical.

Firstly, we'll cover various ways of building views—the pages that control how you see the results prepared by your controllers and models.

Next, you'll see how to create HTML forms quickly, and with built-in safeguards; and you'll also see how to validate your forms.

I'm assuming that readers of this book are familiar with HTML and CSS. The following examples are very simplified, so we can focus on the CI code. And I have assumed that we have already written a CSS file and tucked it away somewhere on our site.

Writing a View

Views control how the user sees your website. They make it easy for you to present a consistent interface, and to change it if you need to. One of the advantages of MVC is that you separate presentation from logic, keeping everything much cleaner.

So far, all we've done is to look at the very simple 'Welcome' view that installs out of the box when you first load CI. (See Chapter 3.) Now let's look at how to make it more elaborate.

A view is just a set of HTML shelves to hold your content. The shelves may be one color or another; there may be lots of little ones, or just a few widely-spaced, elegant ones. But the view doesn't know or care what data is on those shelves. Like certain politicians, it is only interested in presentation.

To create a view, firstly you need to create a skeleton HTML web page as a PHP file. Let's call it `basic_view.php`. Save it in your `application/views` folder. (The reason for saving it in this folder is simply because the loader file looks for it there.)

```
<html>
<head>
</head>
<body>
<p>Hello world!</p>
</body>
</html>
```

Then you just load it from a controller when you want to use it, using `$this->load ->view()` inside an appropriate function:

```
function index()
{
    $this->load->view('basic_view');
}
```

Note that if this were a model or a helper, you'd load it first, and then call it separately when you wanted to use it. With a view, calling it loads it as well, so you only need one line of code.

Of course, that's an empty view. To make it useful, we need content. Say we want to add a title and some text. First we define them in the controller:

```
function index()
{
    $data['mytitle']    = "A website monitoring tool";
    $data['mytext']     = "This website helps you to keep track of the
                          other websites you control.";
}
```

Notice how we have defined them not as separate scalar variables, but as elements of the array `$data` (or any other name we care to give it.). For the first array entry, the 'key' is `'mytitle'` and the 'value' is `"A website monitoring tool"`.

Next, we call the view loading function:

```
function index()
  {
  $data['mytitle']    = "A website monitoring tool";
  $data['mytext']     = "This website helps you to keep track of the
                        other websites you control.";
  $this->load->view('basic_view', $data);
  }
```

We have made the `$data` array into a second parameter of the `$this->load->view()` function, after the name of the view itself. Once the `$data` array reaches the view, CI uses PHP's `extract()` function to turn each element of the `$data` array into a separate variable, with the 'key' as the variable name, and the 'value' as the variable value. These variables can then be referenced directly in our view:

```
<html>
<head>
</head>
<body>
   <h1 class='test'><?php echo $mytitle; ?> </h1>
   <p class='test'><?php echo $mytext; ?> </p>
</body>
</html>
```

You can only pass one variable of data to a view, but by building up an array of arrays, you can pack large amounts of information neatly into that one variable. It seems complicated, but is actually a tightly structured and elegant way of passing information.

Long and Short PHP Syntax

Before we go on, a note about different forms of PHP syntax.

The normal way to include a PHP 'code island' in the midst of HTML code is like this:

```
<?php echo $somevariable ?>
```

However, if you don't like this, CI also supports a shorter version:

```
<?=$somevariable?>
```

In this case, the external brackets delimiting the code island have lost the letters PHP (they are just `<?    ?>`); and `echo` has been replaced by `=`. You can also use shorter syntax for if, for, foreach, and while loops. Complete instructions are in the online User Guide.

Personally, I prefer to stick to the standard format because I'm used to it. If you use the short format, note that some servers won't interpret the abbreviated format correctly. If you still wish to use the short tags, then go to your `config` file, and alter the line:

```
$config['rewrite_short_tags'] = FALSE;
```

to TRUE. CI will then rewrite short tags to the normal form before it sends them to the server. However, if there is a PHP error, using this re-writing function makes the error messages less meaningful, so debugging may be more difficult. As I say, I prefer to stick to the standard format.

For the record, CI also has a 'template parser' class, which allows you to put variables in your HTML code without any actual PHP coding at all. I haven't covered this. It is largely useful if you are working with HTML designers who may be confused by PHP code. Details of this class are available in the User Guide.

Nesting Views

So far, whether we use long or short PHP formats, this is pretty crude HTML. It would be nice, for instance, to put more information in the `<head>` section of the page. Better still if this could be a standard chunk of each page. Once again, something we only have to write (or alter) once, and can then re-use, nesting this view inside other views whenever we need the boring HTML header stuff.

Let's create a page header 'view' for our site, which displays a standard page header, as well as HTML declarations and meta information.

First, we type out the code for our 'nested' header view:

```
<!DOCTYPE html PUBLIC '-//W3C//DTD XHTML 1.0 Strict//EN'http://www.
w3.org/TR/xhtml1/DTD/xhtml1-strict.dtd'><html xmlns='http://www.
w3.org/1999/xhtml'>
<title><?php echo $mywebtitle ?></title>
<base href= <?php echo "$base"; ?> >
<?php echo $myrobots ?>
<link rel="stylesheet" type="text/css" href="<?php echo "$base/
$css;?>">
```

Save this as `views/header_view`. It introduces new variables:

- `$mywebtitle`, which is the page title (the meta tag; this won't show up on the screen, but search engines will read it. It may vary from page to page, so I've made it a variable.)

- `$myrobots`, which I'm using for the standard instruction to robots that this site is not to be indexed.

- `$base and $css`, which describe the base URL and the extra URL for our `.css` file, the stylesheet we're pretending we've already written, which lets us apply formatting consistently. These variables will be generated from data we have already stored in the `CI.config` file. (I could also have used the CI config variable `site_url` instead of `base`.)

What we need to know now is:

- How do we call the second 'nested' view?
- How do we assign values to its variables?

There are two options. Firstly, calls to views can be made from within other views. So our main view, `basic_view`, just needs a new line:

```
<html><head>
<?php $this->load->view('header_view'); ?>
</head><body>
<?php echo $mytitle; ?>
<?php echo $mytext; ?>
</body>
</html>
```

As for the variables, they can be assigned by two new lines in the original controller:

```
function index()
    {
    $data['mytitle']     = "A website monitoring tool";
    $data['mytext']      = "This website helps you to keep track
                            of the other websites you control.";
    $data['myrobots']    = '<meta name="robots" content="noindex
                            ,nofollow">';
    $data['mywebtitle'] = 'Web monitoring tool';
    $data['base']        = $this->config->item('base_url');
    $data['css']         = $this->config->item('css');
    $this->load->view('basic_view', $data);
    }
```

Here the new variables $myrobots, $css, $base, and $mywebtitle are created as new elements of the existing $data array, passed to `basic_view`, which unpacks them, and then made available to `header_view` when this is called by `basic_view`. (Just remember not to use the same variable name in two views that you are nesting, or one will overwrite the other.)

A second way is to add the view from inside the controller, by assigning it to a variable:

```
function index()
    {
    $data['mytitle']     = "A website monitoring tool";
    $data['mytext']      = "This website helps you to keep track of the
                                    other websites you control.";
    $data['myrobots']    = '<meta name="robots" content="noindex,
                                        nofollow">';
```

```
    $data['mywebtitle'] = 'Web monitoring tool';
    $data['base']       = $this->config->item('base_url');
    $data['css']        = $this->config->item('css');
    $data['header']     = $this->load->view('header_view', '', TRUE);
    $this->load->view('basic_view', $data);
}
```

This is probably more correct from a strict MVC perspective.

There are actually three parameters you can pass with the load->view function.

- The first, header_view, is the name of the view to be loaded. This is essential.

- The second, which is optional, is the data to load into it.

- The third is a Boolean value. If you don't specify it, this defaults to FALSE, and the view is sent to the browser. However, if you are nesting the view this way, you want it returned as a string to nest inside the variable you are passing to the host view. Setting the third parameter to TRUE achieves this.

Now we've got a reference to the stylesheet built in, we can update the view to use display classes that we might have defined there:

```
<html><head>
<?php $this->load->view('header_view'); ?>
</head><body>
  <h1 class='test'><?php echo $mytitle; ?> </h1>
  <p class='test'><?php echo $mytext; ?> </p>
</body>
</html>
```

Notice again how CI's MVC system allows you to separate display from content. The views only provide 'shelves' for the content, and even the styling of those shelves is derived from a .css stylesheet.

The view doesn't care what $mytext says, it just displays it on the right shelf with the right formatting. The controller that defines $mytext doesn't even know (or care) how the information it generates is displayed.

So, if we need to change the look of our pages, or display them on a different system (say WAP), then we only need to change one view and one CSS stylesheet. We don't need to mess around inside the code of several controllers.

And if we want to change the information displayed on the page, we don't need to touch the views, and remind ourselves to change some variable in each page we've written. We just change what the controller pushes out.

Remember the 'loose coupling' principle? Once again, this makes it easier to design, upgrade, and maintain your sites.

Practical Issues of Site Architecture

Wait a moment, you're saying in our `header_view`, we generated the CSS stylesheet address dynamically:

```
<link rel="stylesheet" type="text/css" href="<?php echo "$base/
$css";?>">
```

This means that the controller had to produce this data, which is only relevant to how the information is displayed, and we've just said the controller shouldn't know or care about that. Isn't that going right in the face of the 'loose coupling' principle that we had just set out? What's more, generating this information dynamically requires several operations: First, the controller has to look it up in the config file, then the controller has to package it in the `$data` array and pass it to the view, then the view has to extract the single variables `$base` and `$css` and look up their values.

Seems like a roundabout way of doing things. Why not just embed the data statically in the view?

```
<link rel="stylesheet" type="text/css" href="http://www.mysite.com/
mystylesheet.css";">
```

The advantage of building this variable dynamically, despite breaking the MVC 'rule', and despite the overhead of creating variables and passing them around, is that the code is then much more portable. If you move the site, or move your CSS file, you only have to change the code once in the config file, and every controller and view will reflect the change at once. If you hard-code the address in to each view, you'll have to spend time hunting through them for all those absolute URIs you wrote months ago. So which is best?

There isn't a right answer. It depends on what your priorities are. The key is to apply MVC principles sensibly—as a tool rather than a straitjacket. CI allows you a lot of freedom to do this.

A third option—which I use—is to create a special 'display' model. This exists to build the standard page. It puts in headers and CSS file references and so on, and it accepts as a parameter the unique information the file will require. I'll show you this later on in this chapter.

CI's Form Helper: Entering Data

Let's move on to how you use your HTML pages. One of the most important parts of any dynamic site is interaction with the users, and this usually means HTML forms. Writing forms is repetitive and boring.

The CI form helper is a very useful piece of code. It introduces a slightly different syntax, which makes form creation easier. Let's build a form to allow ourselves to enter data on our site about a new website. In a sites table, we want to enter the name, type, and URL of the website, and the date it was updated.

You can build the form as a simple HTML file, or you can build it inside a controller, pack it into a variable, then call a view, and pass the variable to the view. I'm doing the second.

Firstly, we have to load the form helper into the controller where we need to use it. Then, we put the following line in the controller's constructor function:

```
$this->load->helper('form');
```

and of course, we have to start the form.

Now, for the form fields, instead of typing:

```
$variable .= <input type='text' name='name' value=''>
```

CI allows you to enter:

```
$variable .= form_input('name', '');
```

(Remember that 'name' is the title of the field, 'value' is what you want to go into it. Putting something in here gives you a default value, or you can dynamically fetch the existing value from the table.)

Hmm, you say. 33 characters instead of 48, not much of a saving, particularly as I have to load the helper first (another 28 characters). Why bother? Well:

Form Helper Advantage One: Clarity

The first advantage of using the CI form helper is sheer clarity in your code. If you want a more elaborate input box, then in HTML you'd type:

```
$variable = 'input type="text" name="url" id="url" value="www.mysite.
com" maxlength="100" size="50" style="yellow" />';
```

(Remember that type is the sort of box you want—text, hidden, whatever.

`name` is the name that will be used as the key for this value in the POST array.

`id` is so that the box can be referenced on the page, if you're doing neat things with JavaScript.

`value` is the existing or default value that you want the box to show when it comes up on the page.

`maxlength` and `size` are obvious; `style` can be a set of HTML formatting or a reference to a `.css` style defined in your stylesheet.)

CI uses an array instead:

```
$data = array(
            'name'          => 'url',
            'id'            => 'url',
            'value'         => 'www.mysite.com',
            'maxlength'     => '100',
            'size'          => '50',
            'style'         => 'yellow',
        );

$variable = form_input($data);
```

It looks longer, and actually it is: 145 characters as opposed to 110 for the simple HTML. However, it is much clearer, and easier to understand and maintain. This becomes even more obvious if you start to generate some of the values dynamically.

Hidden form fields are very simple. Let's say we want to automatically record the date that our database was updated. We put the date in a `$date` variable, then:

```
form_hidden('updated', $date);
```

If you want a 'text area' box, to give your user more than one line to enter data, say for URLs, which may be quite long, use CI's `form_textarea()` function. If you're happy with a default size, this would simply read:

```
$data = array(
            'name'          => 'url',
            'id'            => 'url',
            'value'         => 'www.mysite.com',
        );

$variable = form_textarea($data);
```

CI's form helper is a great help when you write dropdowns and checkboxes or radio boxes. Let's say we want to change our `'url'` field to a drop-down box, to allow the reader to select one URL from a list of several. First, list the options in an array, then use the `form_dropdown()` function:

```
$urlarray = array(
                   '1'  =>  'www.this.com',
                   '2'  =>  'www.that.com',
                   '3'  =>  'www.theother.com',
               );

$variable = form_dropdown('url', $urlarray, '1');
```

The first value passed to the form, url, is the field name in the site table which we intend to update; the second is the array of options, the third is the key of the option you want to set as default. In other words, if the user accepts the default value, your $_POST array will contain the value 'url => 1', but your user will see the option 'www.this.com'.

Compare this to the plain vanilla HTML, you would otherwise have to write:

```
<select name="type">
<option value="1" selected>www.this.com</option>
<option value="2">www.that.com</option>
<option value="3" >www.theother.com</option>
</select>
```

Now CI's code is actually shorter (128 characters as opposed to 154), as well as much easier to follow.

If you store your list of possible URLs in a separate database table (say it's called 'urls'), then generating a dynamic drop-down box is easy. First generate an array of all possible values:

```
$urlarray      =       array();
$this->db->select('id, url');
$query = $this->db->get('urls');
if ($query->num_rows() > 0)
{
  foreach ($query->result() as $row)
  {
        $urlarray[$row->id] = $row->url;
  }
}
```

then repeat the CI form_dropdown() function we used before:

```
echo form_dropdown('type', $urlarray, '1');
```

Only the contents of $urlarray have changed; this line of code remains the same.

If you are updating an entry rather than creating a new one, you don't want to show your user a default value. You want to show the already existing value for that entry. You should already know the id number of the entry you want to update, so you need to do a database lookup of the 'sites' file first. Make sure you use a different variable name for the second query and the second 'row' variable, or they may overwrite the first set you wrote:

```
$this->db->select('id, url, name');
$this->db->where('id','$id')
$sitequery = $this->db->get('sites');
$siterow = $sitequery->row();
```

Then your CI form drop-down function will read:

```
echo form_dropdown('url', $urlarray, $siterow->url);
```

There isn't room here to go through all the options that the form helper offers. It can handle checkboxes, hidden fields, radio boxes, and others. It is fully explained in CI's online User Guide.

Form Helper Advantage Two: Automation

The second advantage of using the form helper to create your HTML forms is that it automates some things you would otherwise have to script yourself.

Firstly, it intercepts HTML and characters such as quotes, which the user may enter, and escapes them to stop them from breaking the form.

Secondly, it automates links. When you open a form, you have to specify the target page, which will receive the form data and process it. (In CI, this is a function within a controller rather than an actual static page. Let's say the update function of the websites controller.) So, if you were using plain HTML code, you'd write:

```
<form method="post" action="http:/www.mysite.com/index.php/websites/
update" />
```

Whereas, if you open your form with CI, you only need to use:

```
form_open(websites/update)
```

CI automatically works out the base URL from the value in your config file and points the form there. Once again, if you move your site, you won't find that your forms are broken, and have to hunt through for hard-coded URLs to update.

Note incidentally, that CI assumes your forms will always send POST data rather than GET data. CI makes extensive use of the URLs itself, so this avoids confusion.

My 'Display' Model

As promised (and slightly simplified) here is my display model:

```php
<?php
class Display extends Model {

/*create the array to pass to the views*/
    var $data = array();
/*two other class variables*/
    var $base;
    var $status = '';

/*the constructor function: this calls the 'model' parent class, loads
other CI libraries and helpers it requires, and dynamically sets
variables*/
    function Display()
    {
        parent::Model();
        $this->load->helper('form');
        $this->load->library('user_agent');
        $this->load->library('errors');
        $this->load->library('menu');
        $this->load->library('session');

/*now set the standard parts of the array*/
        $this->data['css']  = $this->config->item('css');
        $this->data['base'] = $this->config->item('base_url');
        $this->base         = $this->config->item('base_url');
        $this->data['myrobots'] = '<meta name="robots"
                                    content="noindex,nofollow">';
/*note that CI's session stuff doesn't automatically recall the extra
variables you have added, so you have to look up the user's status in
the ci_sessions table*/
        $sessionid = $this->session->userdata('session_id');
        $this->db->select('status');
        $this->db->where('session_id', $sessionid);
        $query = $this->db->get('ci_sessions');
          if ($query->num_rows() > 0)
              {
              $row = $query->row();
              $this->status = $row->status;
              }
```

```
        }

/*function to assemble a standard page. Any controller can call this.
Just supply as $mydata an array, of key/value pairs for the contents
you want the view to display. Available variables in this view are:
mytitle. menu, mytext, diagnostic
*/
    function mainpage($mydata)
        {
        $this->data['mytitle'] = 'Monitoring website';
        $this->data['diagnostic'] = $diagnostic;
        foreach($mydata as $key => $variable)
        {$this->data[$key] = $variable;}
/*here's the menu class we looked at in Chapter 3*/
        $fred = new menu;
        $this->load->library('session');
        $mysess = $this->session->userdata('session_id');
        if(isset($this->status) && $this->status > 0)
            {$this->data['menu']=
                                $fred->show_menu($this->status);}
        $this->load->view('basic_view', $this->data);

        }

}
?>
```

I can call the main page from any controller with the lines:

```
$this->load->model('display');
$this->display->mainpage($data);
```

and I then know that my view is being assembled dynamically, exactly as I want it.

CI's Validation Class: Checking Data Easily

One chore when you write HTML forms is validating user input. We all know that we should do it, but... So far we've written a simple form, which will trustingly accept any data the user enters. You should always assume that a small minority of your users are malicious, and all the others are stupid. (Just don't tell them.) If they can make a simple mistake, they will. Validating your form tests the information they submit, to make sure it fits rules you specify.

You can do it on the client side, using JavaScript but this is of limited value as a security precaution, as the user can easily circumvent it. Validating the data on the server side means an extra round trip to the server, but it's worth it for the added peace of mind.

It's also quite complex to write the code, but—you guessed it—CI has a validation class that works hand-in-glove with the forms helper to make validation easier.

Let's change our own form submission process to reflect this. You need to make some changes in the form, and also in the function to which it points.

If your form begins with `form_open('sites/update')`, the function you need to modify is the `'update'` function in the `'sites'` controller. If you aren't using the CI form helper, the HTML equivalent is:

```
<form method="post"
action="http:/www.mysite.com/index.php/sites/update" />
```

You need to do three things:

1. Set up validation
2. Set up the controller
3. Set up the forms

Set Up Validation

In the function to which your form points, load the validation library and declare your validation rules:

```
$this->load->library('validation');

$rules['url']        = "required";
$rules['name']       = "required";

$this->validation->set_rules($rules);
```

Each entry must have something in the `'url'` and `'name'` fields. CI gives us various options for specifying what that something should be, and the User Guide explains them in full. They're fairly self-evident: `min_length[6]` obviously means a valid entry in the field must have 6 characters or more, numeric means it must not contain letters, etc. You can also combine rules, using the 'pipe' character to separate them:

```
$rules['name'] = "required|alpha|max_length[12]";
```

would require a `name` of 12 alphabetical characters or less. You can even write your own rules.

Set Up the Controller

Still in the same function, create an 'if/else' loop:

```
if ($this->validation->run() == FALSE)
        {
                $this->load->view('myform');
        }
        else
        {
                $this->load->view('success');
        }
```

You run the validation test, and if the entries don't pass the test, you go back to the entry form. (If you're generating your view in a function inside a controller, say because it has dynamic drop-down fields, then point back to that function instead: `$this->myfunction` **rather than** `$this->load->view('myform');`

If your validation run is successful, create another view (`"success"`) to tell the user that the entry has been accepted, and to give whatever navigation options you want him or her to have to move on.

Set Up the Forms

The entry form that we have built up also needs to be tweaked. Simply returning the user to the form each time an entry doesn't pass the validation tests will make your users really cross! You have to say which field failed, and why. So you have to echo out an extra line somewhere in the form:

```
$this->validation->error_string;
```

This prints out the appropriate messages, and saves the user a lot of frustration.

You also need to arrange for the form fields that were correctly entered to be re-populated with the correct values—otherwise, the user will have to re-enter all the fields each time she or he makes a mistake in one of them. Another way to get her or him really cross!

Firstly, you need to go back to the controller and add some more code. Immediately after the validation rules you set up, create an array of each field you want to re-populate. The array key is the field name as actually used in your table; the array value is what you want the field to be called in the error message:

```
$fields['url'] = 'The URL of your site';
```

Afterwards, add the line:

```
$this->validation->set_fields($fields);
```

Now you've set up an array in the controller to store the existing values, you only need to add lines in your form to echo them back to the user. For a simple text line, this would be:

```
<input type="text" name="url" value="<?php echo $this->validation
->url; ?>" />
```

or, if you're using the CI form helper:

```
$variable .= form_input('url', "$this->validation->url");
```

If this is a new entry form, that should be enough. If you are using the form to update an existing entry, then, the first time the form appears, its value should be whatever it was set to beforehand. (Remember the code example above, where we looked that up and called it `$siterow->url`?)

But say you are using your form to update an existing entry, and it bounces back because one field doesn't validate, you want the value of every other field in your form to be whatever you had changed it to. Otherwise, you'd have to retype the whole form because of one validation error.

This is easily accomplished with an 'either/or' loop. Something like:

```
if(isset($_POST['url']))
    {$myvalue = $this->validation->url;}
else{$myvalue = $siterow->url;}
```

The first time the form appears, there will be nothing in the post array; so you take values from the underlying table. But once you submit it, the post array will be populated, so you take the values from the validation function.

See the CI User Guide for several other things you can do with form validation. You can use it to:

- Automatically prepare your data, e.g., by trimming it or removing potential cross-site scripting attacks
- Write your own complex validation criteria, e.g., that the value the user has entered must not already exist in your database
- Write your own error messages

The validation class is a very useful and powerful part of CI and well worth the time it takes to understand it.

Summary

We've looked at ways in which CI generates 'views', and how it allows you to create 'mini-views', which you can nest inside other views. This means that you can set up a title page, or a part of your display, once, and then use it over and over again, keeping your display separated from your content.

We've also seen how CI helps you through the chore of writing HTML forms, with a set of helpers that simplify the process and cut down on actual coding.

Lastly, we've looked at CI's validation class, which is a powerful tool for keeping an eye on what your users actually try to enter. Nothing's perfect, but this goes a long way towards stopping users form entering rubbish, or trying to exploit security holes in your site. It also looks much more professional when your site politely but firmly catches out user mistakes, rather than silently accepting meaningless entries.

On the way, we've also looked at the MVC process again, and made a choice between the strict application of MVC principles, deliberately breaking these 'rules' to make life easier. CI has a very flexible philosophy: use the tools if you want to, but—provided you understand the issues—feel free to do it some other way if that suits your priorities better.

6
Simplifying Sessions and Security

Enough theory! Now let's begin to write our own application. In this chapter, we'll outline an application that we're going to build, and we'll look at one of the basic questions affecting any website i.e. session management and security.

In this chapter, we'll see:

- How to make your pages secure
- How to use CI's `sessions` class

Starting to Design a Practical Site with CI

We've looked at the CI welcome page and seen how it's built up by a controller file and a view file. That's the equivalent of 'hello world'.

Once upon a time, hobby sites written by amateurs used open-source code and were often regarded as inferior to large 'enterprise' sites written by teams of programmers using complex procedures.

The landscape has changed. Major companies now use open-source technology. For example, NASA and Associated Press use MySQL, the US GAO and even Yahoo are using PHP for certain applications. And I believe that the market for the flexible 'medium sized' application is growing, as large companies realize that their legacy apps can't handle new tasks. It's sometimes easier to build a small, flexible programme than to revise the old one.

CI offers a bridge between 'home-made' code and the structured reliability of 'enterprise' sites. It holds your hand and helps you to program better and produce more consistent and reliable results.

To demonstrate the flexibility of CI, let's build our own application.

To re-state my requirements, I want to build something for a specific purpose. I run several websites, some of them for myself, and some for quite demanding clients. I need to maintain these sites, test them, and generally keep a track of them. Mostly, this is routine stuff. I could hire someone to do it for me, but it would be cheaper to write a website to automate as much of the process as possible.

So my requirements are:

1. To manage one or more remote websites with a minimum of human intervention
2. To run regular tests on the remote sites
3. To generate reports on demand, giving details of the site and of tests conducted

I want to be able to set the site to run on a Cron, if my ISP allows it; if not, to run it myself twice a day or once an hour (as I please), and let it conduct a pre-arranged pattern of tests.

I don't want to know the details, unless something goes wrong (then I'd like an email telling me exactly what happened and exactly where), but I do want to be able to print out management reports for my clients to impress them with the regular and comprehensive checks I'm doing, and the (hopefully!) flawless performance of their sites.

> To avoid making the code too long and repetitive the code in this book is not very secure, so please bear that in mind if you use it for real. This chapter covers a basic means of securing your site's pages against unauthorized users, but other PHP security issues, which aren't unique to CodeIgniter, are outside the scope of this book.

At this stage, we're going to look at CI's approach to things that are generic to most dynamic websites. So we'll leave the detailed design of our site until later. Let's start with some of the very basic items.

Moving Around the Site

Any website is a collection of separate programmes, and it's essential that they are able to talk to each other. As we saw in Chapter 3, CI links them by their URLs. Typically, URLs take the pattern:

base url	http://www.mysite.com. This is the plain vanilla address everyone uses to access your site. Readers don't need to know all the rest of the URL structures because the site builds them up as it needs them.
index file	Segment 1: index.php This is the main file that CI starts off with every time the site is hit.
class (or controller)	Segment 2: start If no controller is set, CI defaults to the controller you specified in the config file—see below.
method (or function)	Segment 3: assessme If no method is set, CI defaults to the index function of the controller, if there is one. If not, you get a '404' page.
plus any parameters	Segment 4: fred (and Segment 5: 12345, Segment 6: hello, etc.)

So, to call the assessme method in the start controller with the parameters fred and 12345, your URL will be:

    http://www.mysite.com.index.php/start/assessme/fred/12345.

This code expects your site to contain a controller called start.php that includes a method assessme, which expects two parameters. A URL like this will call any function in any controller on your site. So it's ideal for a menu-based page.

For a practical example of how this can work, let's set up the first page the user sees on our site. We'll set up a controller called start, and make it our default controller.

Well, first of all, CI, as it comes out of the box, is set to go to the welcome controller by default, so I need to change this. CI's default route is held in the /system/application/config/routes file. At the moment this reads:

    $route['default_controller'] = "welcome";

So I'll change it to:

    $route['default_controller'] = "start";

(Just remember, from the table above, if your default controller doesn't have a default index method, you'll get a 404 error every time anyone logs on to your plain vanilla base URL, which is not a good idea!)

Now I need to write my new start controller. Remember the basic format:

```php
<?php
 class  Start extends Controller
 {
        function Start()
```

```
            {
                        parent::Controller();
            }
            function assessme($name, $password)
            {
                if($name == 'fred' && $password == '12345')
                    {$this->mainpage();}
            }

            }
    ?>
```

Save this in the /system/application/controllers folder as start.php. (Note the cases: Start has an upper-case letter in the class name and constructor function, but not in the saved file name.)

The second line tells you that this is a controller. Then the constructor function starts and loads the parent controller class methods. The assessme function expects two variables $name and $password. CI (from version 1.5 onwards) automatically assigns any URL segments after the second as parameters, so fred and 12345 will become the $name and $password parameters, respectively.

So, if I type in the URL on the previous page, I'll be re-directed to the mainpage() function. We'll set this up later in the start controller. (If not, then the code will just die.)

For those more used to procedural PHP than OO classes, please note a function within a class has to be addressed as $this->xxxx. So, if I'm calling the mainpage() function of the start controller from another function within the start controller, I have to call it $this->mainpage(). Otherwise, CI won't be able to find it.

Of course, it's unlikely that anyone would type in a URL like:

http://www.mysite.com.index.php/start/assessme/fred/12345.

Mostly, they will just enter

http://www.mysite.com

and expect the site to sort out all the internal navigation. So let's start that now.

Often, the first thing you see on a site is a log-in form. So let's prepare one of those. First, I add a new function to my start controller. I want the site to default to this function, so I'll call it index():

```
            function index()
            {
                $data['mytitle']    = "My site";
```

```
$data['base']          = $this->config->item('base_url');
$data['css']           = $this->config->item('css');
$data['mytitle']       = "A website to monitor other websites";
$data['text']          = "Please log in here!";

$this->load->view('entrypage', $data);
}
```

This is calling a view, entrypage. The view includes a form, and the form allows the user to submit a password and username. HTML forms must point to a page that will handle the data in the $_POST array. We've already written the function in our start controller to receive this: it's assessme(). In plain old HTML, the form on our view should begin:

```
<form method="post" action="http:/www.mysite.com/index.php/start/
assessme" />
```

I've explained the assessme function a little. There's not much point in a function that only has one username/password combination. I need some way to look it up in a database. To make the structure more modular, I'm going to hand that over to another function, checkme().

So, as you will see, assessme() calls checkme(). Checkme() does some sort of test on the password and username (we haven't written that yet) and returns 'yes' or 'no' to assessme(). If it's yes, assessme() calls another function, mainpage(), which returns a view.

Notice the advantage of the modular approach. Each function has a role. If I need to alter the way the system checks a password, I only have to alter the checkme() function. If I need to alter the page it displays on a correct response, then I go to the mainpage() function.

Let's just look at the structure of the code and the way the sections interact. (Note that in order to make the example simpler to follow, we are not 'cleaning' the input from our form here. Of course, this leaves your code open to problems. CI's form class automatically sanitizes entered data.

```
/*receives the username and password from the POST array*/

    function assessme()
    {
        $username =        $_POST['username'];
        $password =        $_POST['password'];

    /*calls the checkme function to see if the inputs are OK*/
```

```
        if($this->checkme($username, $password)=='yes')
        {

  /*if the inputs are OK, calls the mainpage function*/
            $this->mainpage();
        }

  /*if they are not OK, goes back to the index function, which
  re-presents the log-in screen */
        else{
            $this->index();
          }
        }

  /*called with a u/n and p/w, this checks them against some list. For
  the moment, there's just one option. Returns 'yes' or 'no'*/

        function checkme($username='', $password='')
        {
          if($username == 'fred' && $password == '12345')
              {return 'yes';

          else{return 'no';}
        }
```

On lines 5-6, `assessme()` receives the output of the form from the `$_POST` array. This will contain something like:

```
[username] => fred [password] => 12345
```

The `assessme()` function passes these two variables to another function, `checkme()`. This simply tests if they are `fred` and `12345`, respectively, and if they are, it returns 'yes'. Obviously, on a real site this would be more complex. You would probably do a database lookup for valid username/password pairs. Making it a separate function means I can test the rest of my code now, and improve the `checkme()` function later, at my leisure.

If the username and password are a valid combination, the `assessme()` function calls another function, `mainpage()`, which lets me into the site. Otherwise, it goes back to showing me the `index()` function—that is, the log-in form again.

The next problem we have is how to manage state. In other words, how to recognize the logged-in user when (s)he makes another page request.

Security/Sessions: Using Another CI Library Class

If I want to build a session mechanism that will keep unwanted users from accessing my files, how many lines of code will it take?

The Internet works by a series of requests. Your browser makes a request to my server to see a particular page. My browser passes the page back to your server. You look at it, and perhaps need to make another request, so you click on a hyperlink, which makes a request to my server. And so on.

The Internet is 'stateless'—that is, each request made by your browser to my website is treated as a separate event, and the HTTP protocol, which underlies the Internet, has no direct way of linking your request to any other requests (that you may have made). It's as if you were in a restaurant, the waiter takes your order, and brings you your meal, but then forgets all about you. That's fine, until he needs to bring you a bill, or to remember that you are entitled to a special discount, or simply remember that you wanted him to ring for a taxi for you after you've finished your meal.

If you want your website to connect one page request with another, you have to manage the 'state' of the relationship: somehow to let the website know that some requests are coming from the same browser, and should be treated specially.

PHP offers two ways of managing state: using cookies, or a specially generated session ID. The PHP session function automatically checks if the website is accepting cookies; if not, it uses the session ID method which is passed via the URL.

 Cookies are small strings of data that websites pass back to any browser that accesses the site. The browser automatically stores it away. Once the cookie is there, the website can check for it when the browser next attempts to access the site. If it finds the right cookie, it can use the information in it to configure itself appropriately. This may mean closing off certain pages to unauthorized users, or adding personal information. In our restaurant analogy, the waiter would leave your bill on the table, and next time he saw you, that would remind him that you were entitled to 15% discount, so he could take that into account when working out your bill.

Because some people set their browsers not to accept cookies, PHP offers an alternative approach. Each time a browser requests access, the site generates a random string called the 'session ID', and returns it to the browser. Browsers then add this to the URL when they make their next request, so that the site can recognize the browser. (Instead of the waiter leaving the bill on your table, you make him carry it back and forth with him to the kitchen.)

CI has a `session` class that handles much of the same stuff. In fact, it reduces a lot of coding to one line. We saw in the last chapter that CI has a wide range of 'library classes', which simplify most of the common tasks that a website deals with. These are the core of frameworks: pre-written chunks of highly abstracted code, which perform essential functions for you. All you need to know is where they are, how to address them and use their methods, and what parameters they expect. In return, you get to use professional code without having to write it!

If you want to use the functionality inside a class from within your controller or model, you must remember to first load the class into the controller or model. (A few classes, such as `config` are always automatically loaded, which is why we haven't loaded it in any of our code so far.)

You load a library class simply:

```
$this->load->library('newclass');
```

Normally, put this line in the constructor of your controller or model.

If you think you will use a library class in every controller, you can have it load automatically just as the `config` class does. Go to the `/system/application/config/autoload` file, and add the name of the class you want into the line:

```
$autoload['libraries'] = array();
```

So that it looks like this:

```
$autoload['libraries'] = array('newclass','oldclass');
```

The library class that we're going to use first is the `session` class, which helps you to maintain state, and to identify users. It's quite simple to do this. Here's our enlarged `assessme()` function from our `start` controller with the new lines highlighted:

```
function assessme()
{
    $this->load->library('session');
    $username    =    $_POST['username'];
    $password    =    $_POST['password'];

  if($this->checkme($username, $password)=='yes')
    {
            $this->mainpage();
    }
  else{$this->index();}
}
```

(I've loaded the `session` library at the start of the function so you can see it, but normally, I'd load it in the controller's constructor, so it is loaded for all the other functions in this class.)

Just loading the session class immediately gives you a huge chunk of functionality in exchange for the one line of code. It will automatically read, create, and update sessions.

Well, to be frank, it's not quite one line of code. You have to make some changes to the `config` file first, to tell the `session` class what you want it to do.

Check your `system/applications/config/config.php` file, and you'll find a section like this:

```
----------------------------------------------------------------------
-----
| Session Variables
|---------------------------------------------------------------------
------
|
| 'session_cookie_name' = the name you want for the cookie
| 'encrypt_sess_cookie' = TRUE/FALSE (boolean).  Whether to encrypt
the cookie
| 'session_expiration'  = the number of SECONDS you want the session
to last.
|  by default sessions last 7200 seconds (two hours).  Set to zero for
no expiration.
|
*/
$config['sess_cookie_name']             = 'ci_session';
$config['sess_expiration']              = 7200;
$config['sess_encrypt_cookie']          = FALSE;
$config['sess_use_database']            = FALSE;
$config['sess_table_name']              = 'ci_sessions';
$config['sess_match_ip']                = FALSE;
$config['sess_match_useragent']         = FALSE;
```

For now, make sure `sess_use_database` is set to FALSE.

Now, every time your users connect, the site will save a cookie on your machine, containing the following information:

- A unique Session ID generated by CI (not to be confused with a PHP session ID string, which isn't generated in this instance). This is a random string created by CI for this session.
- The user's IP Address

- The user's User Agent data (the first 50 characters of the browser data string)
- Timestamps for "last activity"

If you set `sess_encrypt_cookie` to FALSE, you can read the cookie on your browser and see what has been saved (it's partly encoded, but you can make it out) e.g.:

```
ip_address%22%3Bs%3A9%3A%22127.0.0.1%22%3Bs%3A10%3A%22
```

includes the user's URL—in this case, 127.0.0.1). If you set it to TRUE, the cookie is encrypted, just a string of random gunk. Your browser can't even distinguish separate sections of the cookie, which means that the user can't meaningfully alter it without invalidating it.

When the user makes another page request, the site can then check whether the session ID has been saved on the user's browser as part of the cookie. If it has, you know they are part of an existing session. If not, you know they are a new session. Provided I remember to load the CI `session` class on all my other controllers as well, CI will make the same checks for them too. All I have to do is tell each controller how to behave if there isn't a cookie.

Turning Sessions into Security

This in itself doesn't make a security system. Anyone who visits the site starts a session. The code just records whether they are a new visitor or not. One way of preventing unauthorized access to some pages involves adding something else to their cookie if they are 'logged in', so that I can test for that. Then, if they enter the correct username and password once, that will be recorded in the cookie, and the session mechanism will find it when it checks for cookies as each new request comes through. I can then test for that, and if I find it, the site will let them into protected pages for the rest of the session. They won't have to keep on logging in.

Adding something to the cookie is easy. In my `assessme()` controller, once I have decided if the password and username are acceptable, I add:

```
if($this->checkme($username, $password)=='yes')
{
    $newdata = array(
                        'status' => 'OK',
                    );
    $this->session->set_userdata($newdata);
    $this->mainpage();
}
```

That takes the contents of my `$newdata` array—just one variable in this case—and adds it to the cookie string. Now, whenever the password/username combination is acceptable, `assessme()` will add `'OK'` to the cookie, and I can start each controller with this code:

```
/*remember to load the library!*/
    $this->load->library('session');
/*look for a 'status' variable in the contents of the session cookie*/
$status = $this->session->userdata('status');
/*if it's not there, make the user log in*/
    if(!isset($status) || $status != 'OK')
            { /*function to present a login page again...*/}
/*otherwise, go ahead with the code*/
```

Here, you have the basis of a security fence around your site. You can easily make it more elaborate. For instance, if some of your users have higher access levels than others, you can store a level in the status variable rather than `'OK'`—then you can use this in conditional tests to control access to functions.

Saving this sort of data in a cookie is frowned upon because the user can easily rewrite the cookie on their machine between visits to your site. Given that CI's session class encrypts it, you're fairly safe. However, the alternative is to create a database of users, and after one has logged in, to write the `'OK'` to the database against that session ID. Then, for subsequent accesses, you check the session ID (in the cookie) against the database, to see whether it has `'OK'` or a level against it.

It is very simple to save the session data in your database. First, create the database table. If you're using MySQL, use this SQL query:

```
CREATE TABLE IF NOT EXISTS  `ci_sessions` (
session_id varchar(40) DEFAULT '0' NOT NULL,
ip_address varchar(16) DEFAULT '0' NOT NULL,
user_agent varchar(50) NOT NULL,
last_activity int(10) unsigned DEFAULT 0 NOT NULL,
status varchar(5) DEFAULT 'no',
PRIMARY KEY (session_id)
);
```

Then, alter the connection parameters in the `system/application/config/database.php` file to tell CI where the database is. See Chapter 4 for more details on databases.

If all works, you will see the data build up in your database table as you connect and disconnect. If you have sessions stored in a database table, as each user connects to your site, the site tests for a cookie. If it finds one, you can then have it read the session id, and match this against the session ids stored in the database.

You now have a robust session mechanism. And all of this came from one line of code!

Just one caveat. The native PHP session class can cope with users who turn off cookies on their browsers. (Instead of storing a cookie, it adds session data to the URL string.) The CI class does not do this. If the user has turned off cookies, then (s)he can't log on to your site. Whether this is a problem for you depends on the people you expect to use your site. This is one enhancement I hope Rick Ellis will soon make to CI.

Security

Notice that the session class automatically stores information about the IP address and user agent of the user making a page request. You can use these to give additional security.

There are two settings you can change in your config file for additional security:

- **sess_match_ip**: If you set this to true, CI will attempt to match the user's IP address when it reads the session data. This is to prevent users from 'hijacking' a log-in. However, some servers (both ISPs and large corporate servers) may issue requests by the same end user over different IP addresses. If you set this value to true, you may exclude them unintentionally.

- **sess_match_useragent**: If you set this to true, CI will try to match the User Agent when reading the session data. This means that someone who tried to hijack a session would have to ensure that the 'user agent' setting returned by his or her system matched that of the genuine user. It makes hijacking a little more difficult.

CI also has a user_agent class, which you load like this:

```
$this->load->library('user_agent');
```

Once loaded, you can ask it to return various information about any agent browsing your site, for instance, the type of browser and operating system, and in particular whether it is a browser, mobile, or robot. If you want to list the robots that visit your site, you might do it like this:

```
$fred = $this->agent->is_robot();
if ($fred == TRUE)
    {$agent = $this->agent->agent_string();
/*add code here to store or analyse the name the user agent is
returning*/
}
```

The class works by loading, and comparing against, the array of user agents, browsers, and robots contained in another of the `config` files: `system/application/config/user_agents`.

If you wished, you could easily develop this to enable your site to lock out certain types of browser or certain robots. However, remember that it is easy for an attacker to write robot user agents, and have them return whatever `user_agent` string you want, so they can easily masquerade as common browsers. Many robots, including ones like the Googlebot listed in CI's `user_agents` array, are 'well-behaved'. This means that if you set your `robots.txt` file to exclude them, they won't trespass. There is no easy way of excluding robots that don't obey this file, unless you know their names in advance!

In CI, the session mechanism stores the IP of the requesting site, so you could use this to operate a black-list of sites. Retrieve the IP from the session like this:

```
/*remember to load the library!*/
   $this->load->library('session');
/*look for an 'ip_address' variable in the contents of the session
cookie*/
$ip = $this->session->userdata('ip_address');
```

Then you can test the `$ip` variable against a blacklist.

You could also develop CI's session mechanism to limit the damage from repeated requests—such as denial of service attacks where a robot is set to overload your site by repeatedly asking for pages. Or you could use this mechanism to handle 'dictionary' attacks, where a robot is set up to call your log-in form repeatedly, and try hundreds or thousands of password/username combinations until it finds the right one.

You can do this because CI's sessions class stores the `last_activity` time for each session. Each time a page is requested, you can check how long ago the last request was made by this user. While one time interval doesn't tell you very much, you can set the system to store more data and to develop usage patterns. A dictionary attack relies on getting a speedy reply, otherwise it will take too long. If you detected too many requests in rapid succession, you could either end the session, or slow down the response.

Summary

We've outlined an application that we'd like to build, and attacked the first issue that almost any application raises: session management and (if we want to protect parts of our site from unauthorized users) security.

To do this, we've looked at the CI `sessions` class in some detail, and seen how it creates session records and leaves cookies on the visitor's browser.

It can then look for cookies when subsequent requests are made, and you can use the response to control the way your site responds.

7
CodeIgniter and Objects

This is the geek chapter. It describes the way CodeIgniter actually works, 'under the hood'. If you are new to CI, you may want to skip it. However, sooner or later, you may want to understand why things happen in certain ways—as opposed to just knowing that they do.

Objects confused me when I started to use CodeIgniter. I came to CodeIgniter via PHP 4, which is a procedural language, not really an Object-Oriented (OO) language. I duly looked up objects and methods, properties and inheritance, and encapsulation, but my early attempts to write CI code were plagued by the error message "Call to a member function on a non-object". I saw it so often that I was thinking of having it printed on a t-shirt: it has a mysteriously libertarian, anarchist tone, and I could see myself wearing it at a modern art exhibition.

To save the world from a lot of boring t-shirts, this chapter covers the way in which CI uses objects, and the different ways you can write and use your own objects. Incidentally, I've used 'variables/properties', and 'methods/functions' interchangeably, as CI and PHP often do. You write 'functions' in your controllers for instance, when the OO purist would call them 'methods'. You define class 'variables' when the purist would call them 'properties'.

Object-Oriented Programming

I'm assuming you—like me—have a basic knowledge of OOP, but may have learned it as an afterthought to 'normal' PHP 4. PHP 4 is not an OO language, though some OO functionality has been tacked on to it. PHP 5 is much better, with an underlying engine that was written from the ground up with OO in mind.

But you can do most of the basics in PHP 4, and CI manages to do everything it needs internally, in either language.

The key thing to remember is that, when an OO program is running, there is always one current object (but only one). Objects may call each other and hand over control to each other, in which case the current object changes; but only one of them can be current at any one time. The current object defines the 'scope'—in other words, which variables (properties) and methods (functions) are available to the program at that moment. So it's important to know, and control, which object is current. Like police officers and London buses, variables and methods belonging to objects that aren't current just aren't there for you when you most need them.

PHP, being a mixture of functional and OO programming, also offers you the possibility that no object is current! You can start off as a functional program, call an object, let it take charge for a while, and then let it return control to the program. Luckily, CI takes care of this for you.

Working of the CI 'Super-Object'

CI works by building one 'super-object': it runs your whole program as one big object, in order to eliminate scoping issues.

When you start CI, a complex chain of events occurs. If you set your CI installation to create a log, you'll see something like this:

```
 1 DEBUG - 2006-10-03 08:56:39 --> Config Class Initialized
 2 DEBUG - 2006-10-03 08:56:39 --> No URI present. Default controller
                                   set.
 3 DEBUG - 2006-10-03 08:56:39 --> Router Class Initialized
 4 DEBUG - 2006-10-03 08:56:39 --> Output Class Initialized
 5 DEBUG - 2006-10-03 08:56:39 --> Input Class Initialized
 6 DEBUG - 2006-10-03 08:56:39 --> Global POST and COOKIE data
                                   sanitized
 7 DEBUG - 2006-10-03 08:56:39 --> URI Class Initialized
 8 DEBUG - 2006-10-03 08:56:39 --> Language Class Initialized
 9 DEBUG - 2006-10-03 08:56:39 --> Loader Class Initialized
10 DEBUG - 2006-10-03 08:56:39 --> Controller Class Initialized
11 DEBUG - 2006-10-03 08:56:39 --> Helpers loaded: security
12 DEBUG - 2006-10-03 08:56:40 --> Scripts loaded: errors
13 DEBUG - 2006-10-03 08:56:40 --> Scripts loaded: boilerplate
14 DEBUG - 2006-10-03 08:56:40 --> Helpers loaded: url
15 DEBUG - 2006-10-03 08:56:40 --> Database Driver Class Initialized
16 DEBUG - 2006-10-03 08:56:40 --> Model Class Initialized
```

On startup—that is, each time a page request is received over the Internet—CI goes through the same procedure. You can trace the log through the CI files:

1. The `index.php` file receives a page request. The URL may indicate which controller is required, if not, CI has a default controller (line 2). `Index.php` makes some basic checks and calls the `codeigniter.php` file (`\codeigniter\codeigniter.php`).

2. The `codeigniter.php` file instantiates the Config, Router, Input, URL, (etc.) classes (lines 1, and 3 to 9). These are called the 'base' classes: you rarely interact directly with them, but they underlie almost everything CI does.

3. `codeigniter.php` tests to see which version of PHP it is running on, and calls Base4 or Base5 (`/codeigniter/Base4(or 5).php`). These create a 'singleton' object: one which ensures that a class has only one instance. Each has a public `&get_instance()` function. Note the `&:`, this is assignment by reference. So if you assign to the `&get_instance()` method, it assigns to the single running instance of the class. In other words, it points you to the same pigeonhole. So, instead of setting up lots of new objects, you are starting to build up one 'super-object', which contains everything related to the framework.

4. After a security check, `codeigniter.php` instantiates the controller that was requested, or a default controller (line 10). The new class is called `$CI`. The function specified in the URL (or a default) is then called, and life as we know it starts to wake up and happen. Depending on what you wrote in your controller, CI will then initialize any other classes you need, and 'include' functional scripts you asked for. So in the log above, the model class is initialized. (line 16) The 'boilerplate' script, on the other hand, which is also shown in the log (line 13), is one I wrote to contain standard chunks of text. It's a `.php` file, saved in the `scripts` folder, but it's not a class: just a set of functions. If you were writing 'pure' PHP you might use 'include' or 'require' to bring it into the namespace: CI needs to use its own 'load' function to bring it into the super-object.

The concept of 'namespace' or scope is crucial here. When you declare a variable, array, object, etc., PHP holds the variable name in its memory and assigns a further block of memory to hold its contents. However, problems might arise if you define two variables with the same name. (In a complex site, this is easily done.) For this reason, PHP has several sets of rules. For example:

- Each function has its own namespace or scope, and variables defined within a function are usually 'local' to it. Outside the function, these are meaningless.

- You can declare 'global' variables, which are held in a special global namespace and are available throughout the program.
- Objects have their own namespaces: variables exist inside the object for as long as the object exists, but can only be referenced through the object.

So `$variable`, global `$variable`, and `$this->variable` are three different things.

Particularly, before OO, this could lead to all sorts of confusion: you may have too many variables in your namespace (so that conflicting names overwrite each other), or you may find that some variables are just not accessible from whatever scope you happen to be in. CI offers a clever way of sorting this out for you.

So, now you've started CI, using the URL `www.mysite.com/index.php/welcome/index`, which specifies that you want the `index` function of the `welcome` controller.

If you want to see what classes and methods are now in the current namespace and available to you, try inserting this 'inspection' code in the `welcome` controller:

```
$fred = get_declared_classes();
foreach($fred as $value)
{$extensions = get_class_methods($value);
    print "class is $value, methods are: ";
    print_r($extensions);}
```

When I ran this just now, it listed 270 declared classes. Most are other libraries declared in my installation of PHP. The last 11 came from CI: ten were the CI base classes (config, router, etc.) and last of all came the controller class I had called. Here's the last 11, with the methods omitted from all but the last two:

```
258: class is CI_Benchmark
259: class is CI_Hooks,
260: class is CI_Config,
261: class is CI_Router,
262: class is CI_Output,
263: class is CI_Input,
264: class is CI_URI,
265: class is CI_Language,
266: class is CI_Loader,
267: class is CI_Base,
268: class is Instance,
269: class is Controller, methods are: Array ( [0] => Controller [1]
=> _ci_initialize [2] => _ci_load_model [3] => _ci_assign_to_models
[4] => _ci_autoload [5] => _ci_assign_core [6] => _ci_init_scaffolding
[7] => _ci_init_database [8] => _ci_is_loaded [9] => _ci_scaffolding
[10] => CI_Base )
270: class is Welcome, methods are: Array ( [0] => Welcome [1] =>
```

```
index [2] => Controller [3] => _ci_initialize [4] => _ci_load_model
[5] => _ci_assign_to_models [6] => _ci_autoload [7] => _ci_assign_core
[8] => _ci_init_scaffolding [9] => _ci_init_database [10] => _ci_is_
loaded [11] => _ci_scaffolding [12] => CI_Base )
```

Notice—in parentheses as it were—that the `Welcome` class (number 270: the controller I'm using) has all the methods of the `Controller` class (number 269). This is why you always start off a controller class definition by extending the `controller` class—you need your controller to inherit these functions. (And similarly, models should always extend the `model` class.) `Welcome` has two extra methods: `Welcome` and `index`. So far, out of 270 classes, these are the only two functions I wrote!

Notice also that there's an Instance class. If you inspect the class variables of the 'Instance' class, you will find there are a lot of them! Just one class variable of the Instance class, taken almost at random, is the array `input`:

```
["input"]=> &object(CI_Input)#6 (4) { ["use_xss_clean"]=> bool(false)
["ip_address"]=> bool(false) ["user_agent"]=> bool(false) ["allow_get_
array"]=> bool(false)  }
```

Remember when we loaded the input file and created the original input class? Its class variables were:

```
use_xss_clean is bool(false)
ip_address is bool(false)
user_agent is bool(false)
allow_get_array is bool(false)
```

As you see, they have now all been included within the 'instance' class.

All the other CI 'base' classes (router, output, etc.) are included in the same way. You are unlikely to need to write code referencing these base classes directly, but CI itself needs them to make your code work.

Copying by Reference

You may have noticed that the CI_Input class is assigned by reference (`["input"]=> &object(CI_Input)`). This is to ensure that as its variables change, so will the variables of the original class. As assignment by reference can be confusing, here's a short explanation. We're all familiar with simple copying in PHP:

```
$one      =      1;
$two      =      $one;
echo $two;
```

produces 1, because $two is a copy of $one. However, if you re-assign $one:

```
$one      =      1;
$two      =      $one;
$one      =      5;
echo $two;
```

This code still produces 1, because changes to $one after $two has been assigned aren't reflected in $two. This was a one-off assignment of the value that happened to be in variable $one at the time, to a new variable $two, but once it was done, the two variables led separate lives. (In just the same way, if I alter $two, $one doesn't change.)

In effect, PHP creates two pigeonholes: one called $one, one called $two. A separate value lives in each. You may, on any one occasion, make the values equal, but after that they each do their own thing.

PHP also allows copying 'by reference'. If you add just a simple & to line 2 of the code:

```
$one      =      1;
$two      =&     $one;
$one      =      5;
echo $two;
```

Then the code now echoes 5: the change we made to $one has also happened to $two.

Changing the = to =& in the second line means that the assignment is 'by reference'. Now, it's as if there was only one pigeonhole, which has two names ($one and $two). Whatever happens to the contents of the pigeonhole happens both to $one and to $two, as if they were just different names for the same thing.

The principle works for objects as well as simple string variables. You can copy or clone an object using the = operator, in which case you make a simple one-off new copy, which then leads an independent life. Or, you can assign one to the other by reference: now the two objects point to each other, so any changes made to the one will also happen to the other. Again, think of them as two different names for the same thing.

Adding Your own Code to the CI 'Super-Object'

You contribute to the process of building the 'super-object' as you write your own code. Suppose you have written a model called 'status', which contains two class variables of its own, $one and $two, and a constructor that assigns them values of 1 and 2 respectively. Let's examine what happens when you load this model.

The 'instance' class includes a variable 'load', which is a copy (by reference) of the object CI_Loader. So the code you write in your controller is:

```
$this->load->model($status)
```

In other words, take the class variable 'load' of the current CI super-class ('this') and use its method 'model'. This actually references the 'model' function in the 'loader' class (`/system/libraries/loader.php`) and that says:

```
function model($model, $name = '')
{
    if ($model == '')
        return;

    $obj =& get_instance();
    $obj->_ci_load_model($model, $name);
}
```

(The $name variable in this code is there in case you want to load your model under an alias. I don't know why you should want to do this; perhaps it's wanted by the police in several other namespaces.)

As you can see, the model is loaded by reference into the Instance class. Because get_instance() is a singleton method, you're always referencing the same instance of the Instance class.

If you run the controller again, using our 'inspect' code modified to show class variables, you'll now see that the instance class contains a new class variable:

```
["status"]=> object(Status)#12 (14) { ["one"]=> int(1) ["two"]=>
int(2) ... (etc)
```

In other words, the CI 'super-object' now includes an object called $status that includes the class variables you defined in your original status model, assigned to the values we set.

So we are gradually building up the one big CI 'super-object', which allows you to use any of its methods and variables without worrying too much about where they came from and what namespace they might be in.

This is the reason for the CI arrow syntax. To use the methods of (say) a model, you must first load the model in your controller:

```
$this->load->model('Model_name');
```

This makes the model into a class variable of `$this->`, the current (controller) class. You then call a function of that class variable from the controller, like this:

```
$this->Model_name->function();
```

and off you go.

Problems with the CI 'Super-Object'

There was one big problem for Rick Ellis when he wrote the original code. PHP 4 handles objects less elegantly than PHP 5, so he had to introduce a 'really ugly hack' (his words) into the Base4 file. Ugly or not, the hack works, and so we don't need to worry about it. It just means that CI works as well on PHP 4 systems as it does on PHP 5.

There are two other issues worth mentioning here:

- You can find yourself trying to work with an object that isn't available.
- You have to structure your site carefully, because you can't call methods of one controller from inside another.

Let's look at these two problems in turn. You remember the t-shirt I mentioned above: "Call to a member function on a non-object"? This annoying error message often means that you tried to use a function from a class (say a model class that you wrote) but forgot to load the class. In other words, you wrote:

```
$this->Model_name->function();
```

but forgot to precede it by:

```
$this->load->model('Model_name');
```

Or some variation of this: for instance, you loaded the model inside one function of a class, which loads the model, but only inside that function, and then you tried to use its methods from inside another function, albeit in the same class. It's usually best to load models, etc., from the class constructor function: then they are available to all the other functions in the class.

The problem can also be more subtle. If you write your own classes, for instance, you may wish to use them to access the database, or to look up something in your `config` files—in other words, to give them access to something that is part of the CI 'super-object'. (There's a fuller discussion of how to add your own classes or libraries in Chapter 13.) To summarize, unless your new class is a controller, a model, or a view, it doesn't get built in to the CI super-object. So you can't write things inside your new class like this:

```
$this->config->item('base_url);
```

This just won't work, because to your new class, `$this->` means itself, not the CI super-object. Instead, you have to build your new class into the super-class by calling the Instance class (sound familiar?) using another variable name (usually `$obj`)

```
$obj =& get_instance();
```

Now you can write that call to the CI superclass as:

```
$obj->config->item('base_url);
```

and this time it works.

However, as you write your new class, remember that it still has its own identity. Let's use a short outline example to make this clearer.

You want to write a library class that prepares a URL based on the location of the server that requests the page. So you write some code to look up the geographic location of the IP address that is calling your page (using a library like the netGeo class available from `http://www.phpclasses.org/browse/package/514.html`). Then, using a switch function, you select one of several alternative functions, and you serve up an English page to US or British requests, a German page to German or Austrian requests, and so on. Now, the full URL to your country-specific page will be made up of two parts: the base URL of your site (`www.mysite.com/index.php/`), plus the URL of the individual page (`mypage/germanversion`).

You need to get the base URL of the site from CI's `config` file. The second half of the URL is being generated by a switch statement in the constructor of your new class—if this client is in Germany, serve up the German page function, etc. As this is being done in the constructor calls, you need to put the result into a class variable, so it can be used in other functions within the same class. This means that:

- The first half of your URL comes from the CI `config` file, which can only be referenced through the superobject, to which you have linked using `$obj =& get_instance()`. In other words, you call it using `$obj->config->item('base_url');`

- But the second half of your URL is generated inside the constructor of your new class and assigned to a class variable, $base. It has nothing to do with the CI super-object; it belongs to your new class, and is referenced as $this->base

This can lead to using both $this-> and $obj-> references in the same line—e.g.:

```
class my_new_class{
var $base;
My_new_class()
{
$obj =& get_instance();
// geolocation code here, returning a value through a switch statement
//this value is assigned to $local_url
$this->base = $obj->config->item('base_url);
$this->base .= $local_url;
}
```

Getting these confused is another fruitful source of, "Call to a member function on a non-object". In our example, you'd get that error message if you tried to call either $obj->base, or $this->config->item().

Turning to the remaining problem, you can't call methods of one controller from inside another. Why would you want to do this? Well, it depends. In one application, I wrote a series of self-test functions inside each controller. If I called $this->selftest() inside the controller, it did various useful tests. But it seemed against the principle programming virtue of laziness to have to repeatedly call the self-test method in each controller separately. I tried to write one function, in one controller, that would go through all the controllers, call the self-test method in each, amalgamate all the results while I stared out of the window, and then give me a comprehensive report in exchange for only one mouse click. Alas, no. Can't be done.

As a general rule, if you have code that may be needed by more than one controller, put it in a model or a separate script of some sort. Then they can both use it. (Of course, this doesn't help with my self-test problem, because the code to test the controllers has to be in the controllers!)

But these are minor problems. As Rick Ellis put it to me:

"I wanted to arrive at something more simple so I decided to make one big controller object containing lots of other object instances:…when a user creates their own controllers they can easily access anything that has been instantiated just by calling it, without worrying about scope".

That's pretty well how it works, most of the time, efficiently, and completely in the background. So I never did get that t-shirt printed.

Summary

We've looked at the way CI builds up one 'super-object' to make sure that all the methods and variables you need are automatically available to you without you having to manage them and worry about their scope.

CI makes extensive use of assignment by reference, instantiating one class after another and linking them all together so that you can access them through the 'super-class'. Most of the time, you don't need to know what the 'super-class' is doing, provided that you use CI's 'arrow' notation correctly.

We've also looked at how you can write your own classes and still have access to the CI framework.

Lastly, we looked at a few problems that can arise, particularly if you're not used to OO programs, and suggested a few solutions.

8

Using CI to Test Code

This chapter looks at how CI can help you to test your code. Testing is the heart of our application. We've built it to test other remote applications; we also want to test it itself, as we develop it. CI makes this a lot easier.

However, 'testing' can mean a lot of things, so we start off by looking at the difference between the two main types, and at some other reasons for which you might want to run tests.

Then we look at CI classes to help with testing:

- Unit tests
- Benchmarking
- The 'profiler'
- Ways in which CI helps you to involve your database in tests without scrambling live data

Why Test, and What For?

A lot has been written about testing. It has become an industry. Complex programs employ an army of testers or test software. And the concept of 'test-driven development' is that you design your tests first, before even a single line of code: then write your code to pass them.

At the other extreme, many programmers don't do any systematic testing, because it seems too difficult, boring, or time-consuming. Maybe we try the program out a few times, and then hope for the best.

CI offers several ways to make testing easier. Even—honestly!—more fun.

There are two main types of tests:

- Unit tests: These take a 'bottom-up' approach. They look at one chunk of your code, say a single function, throw in some variables, and see if it gives back the right answer.

- End-to-end tests: These are 'top-down'. They focus on something the site is supposed to do, and see if it does it: for instance, they try to log in to your site (using a valid username and password) and see if it allows them. (And then they try to log in using an invalid password…)

As you can see, it's a different philosophy. One tests chunks of code, and doesn't know or care what the end result is; while the other tests the end result, and doesn't know or care which chunks of code got you there.

The important thing is to think through why you are testing. What worries you most? What is most likely to go wrong and embarrass you? What sort of information do you need back from your tests—just a simple OK/ not OK, or something more complex? For each application, how much time can you afford to put in to writing and maintaining tests?

While we're developing our test site, we need to test our code while we write it. Of course, we try to anticipate everything the user might do, and every situation that might arise. This is one big area where unit tests are useful: just the fact of designing tests helps you to improve the design of the code.

Once our code is up on a production server, its day-to-day integrity is largely beyond our control. At its worst, this leads to clients finding error messages or blank screens, and expecting you to do something about it, often at times when you'd rather be doing something else. That's why we're building this site, to test other remote sites.

CI can help us to check developing sites to see:

- Firstly, that we've anticipated a range of things that might go wrong. For instance, I might do a database query to delete a record with a given ID number in a specific table. Yes, it works: I've tested it by doing it. But what happens if—somehow—the code calls a table that doesn't exist? Or gives an invalid ID number? Or doesn't give one at all? This is where unit tests are helpful.

- Secondly, when I write more code somewhere else, does my first block of code still work the way I want, or have I inadvertently altered something the first block depends on? Again, a job for unit tests. They can also help us to check production sites regularly to see that the site is there (and all the parts of it—e.g., if the database is on a separate server, an ordinary 'ping' test won't do!)

CI gives you a lot of help, whichever position you take. It doesn't have a class to run end-to-end tests, but you can do this using other PHP code that is outside the scope of this book. But let's look first of all at how CI displays errors to you as you develop code.

CI's Error Handling Class

CI has a system of its own for detecting and reporting errors. In one way, these are the simplest and most common tests of all: they are those helpful (or infuriating) messages you see when you are developing your own code and it doesn't work.

By default, CI displays all errors on the screen. The alternative is to fail silently; giving you no idea of what went wrong, so this is essential for development. Overall behavior is controlled from the main index.php file, which begins:

```
/*
|--------------------------------------------------------------
| PHP ERROR REPORTING LEVEL
|--------------------------------------------------------------
|
| By default CI runs with error reporting set to ALL.  For security
| reasons you are encouraged to change this when your site goes live.
| For more info visit:  http://www.php.net/error_reporting
|
*/
    error_reporting(E_ALL);
```

This is a PHP command. To turn off error reporting, replace the last line with:

```
error_reporting(0);
```

This would be appropriate for a production site, where you don't want the details of errors displayed to users.

CI has three functions, show_error(), show_404(), and log_message(), which control how errors are displayed on your system. (Unusually, these functions are globally available: you don't have to load anything before you can use them, just go right ahead and type them in!). In fact, show_error() and show_404() usually happen by default; the first displays your errors in a neat little HTML-formatted box at the top of the screen; and the second shows a '404' page' if you try to access a page that isn't there.

The third function, `log_message()`, is more interesting. You may want to develop your own error log, maybe because you can't access the log on your ISP's Apache server. First, you need to set permissions to make sure that your `/system/logs` folder is writable. Then you set the level of logging in the `config` file:

```
/*
|------------------------------------------------------------------
------
| Error Logging Threshold
|------------------------------------------------------------------
----
|
| If you have enabled error logging, you can set an error threshold to
| determine what gets logged. Threshold options are:
|
|  0 = Disables logging
|  0 = Error logging TURNED OFF
|  1 = Error Messages (including PHP errors)
|  2 = Debug Messages
|  3 = Informational Messages
|  4 = All Messages
|
| For a live site you'll usually only enable Errors (1) to be logged
| otherwise your log files will fill up very fast.
|
*/
$config['log_threshold'] = 4;

/*
```

This starts logging, automatically.

If you alter `index.php` to turn off the screen display of messages, this doesn't stop logging. So you can see what your system is doing, and your users can't.

CI generates a new log file each day, and writes to it as you instruct it. But beware, these log files can rapidly become very large. Here's a sample of one:

```
33 DEBUG - 2006-12-30 19:58:04 --> Language Class Initialized
34 DEBUG - 2006-12-30 19:58:04 --> Language file loaded: language/english/db_lang.php
35 DEBUG - 2006-12-30 19:58:22 --> Config Class Initialized
36 DEBUG - 2006-12-30 19:58:22 --> Hooks Class Initialized
37 DEBUG - 2006-12-30 19:58:22 --> No URI present. Default controller set.
38 DEBUG - 2006-12-30 19:58:22 --> Router Class Initialized
39 DEBUG - 2006-12-30 19:58:22 --> Output Class Initialized
40 DEBUG - 2006-12-30 19:58:22 --> Input Class Initialized
41 DEBUG - 2006-12-30 19:58:22 --> Global POST and COOKIE data sanitized
42 DEBUG - 2006-12-30 19:58:22 --> URI Class Initialized
43 DEBUG - 2006-12-30 19:58:22 --> Language Class Initialized
44 DEBUG - 2006-12-30 19:58:22 --> Loader Class Initialized
45 DEBUG - 2006-12-30 19:58:22 --> Session Class Initialized
46 DEBUG - 2006-12-30 19:58:22 --> Encrypt Class Initialized
47 DEBUG - 2006-12-30 19:58:23 --> Database Driver Class Initialized
48 DEBUG - 2006-12-30 19:58:23 --> A session cookie was not found.
49 DEBUG - 2006-12-30 19:58:23 --> Controller Class Initialized
50 DEBUG - 2006-12-30 19:58:23 --> Model Class Initialized
51 DEBUG - 2006-12-30 19:58:23 --> Helpers loaded: form
52 DEBUG - 2006-12-30 19:58:23 --> Table Class Initialized
53 DEBUG - 2006-12-30 19:58:24 --> Model Class Initialized
54 DEBUG - 2006-12-30 19:58:24 --> FTP Class Initialized
55 DEBUG - 2006-12-30 19:58:24 --> Helpers loaded: url
56 DEBUG - 2006-12-30 19:58:24 --> Model Class Initialized
57 DEBUG - 2006-12-30 19:58:24 --> Helpers loaded: date
58 DEBUG - 2006-12-30 19:58:24 --> Model Class Initialized
59 DEBUG - 2006-12-30 19:58:24 --> Model Class Initialized
60 DEBUG - 2006-12-30 19:58:24 --> Helpers loaded: form
61 DEBUG - 2006-12-30 19:58:24 --> Helpers loaded: url
62 DEBUG - 2006-12-30 19:58:25 --> Unit Testing Class Initialized
63 DEBUG - 2006-12-30 19:58:25 --> Validation Class Initialized
```

—and so on for another 3000 lines, on a day when the program had only limited usage.

In practice, you may want to develop your own error handling procedures to display a default message to users when something goes wrong.

CI's Unit Test Class

Now let's get on to proper testing: proactively looking at bits of your code to make sure they work under different circumstances.

CI makes unit testing simple with its own class. You load it with this:

```
$this->load->library('unit_test');
```

and then, for each test, you decide three variables:

- $test—the actual test, as a PHP expression
- $expected_result—the result you expect
- $test_name—the test name as you want it displayed

Here are two tests of the PHP function `floor()` (which rounds down a 'float' number to the nearest integer below it). Notice that the first expected result is correct; the second is wrong. (A deliberate mistake, honestly.)

```
$test = floor(1.56);
$expected_result = 1;
$test_name = 'tests php floor function';
$this->unit->run($test, $expected_result, $test_name);
$test = floor(2.56);
$expected_result = 1;
$test_name = 'tests php floor function';
$this->unit->run($test, $expected_result, $test_name);
```

adding:

```
echo $this->unit->report();
```

displays the result as formatted HTML, like this:

Test Name	tests php floor function
Test Datatype	Float
Expected Datatype	Integer
Result	Passed
File Name	E:\xampplite\htdocs\packt2\system\application\controllers\tests.php
Line Number	108

Test Name	tests php floor function
Test Datatype	Float
Expected Datatype	Integer
Result	Failed
File Name	E:\xampplite\htdocs\packt2\system\application\controllers\tests.php
Line Number	113

If you want your system to analyze or store it, using:

```
echo $this->unit->result();
```

returns the information as a two-dimensional array, which you can use:

```
Array (
    [0] => Array
      ( [Test Name] => tests php floor function
        [Test Datatype ] => Float
```

```
        [Expected Datatype] => Integer
        [Result] => Passed
        [File Name] => E:\myfile.php [Line Number] => 69 )
  [1] => Array
        ( [Test Name] => tests php floor function
        [Test Datatype ] => Float
        [Expected Datatype] => Integer
        [Result] => Failed
        [File Name] => E:\myfile.php
        [Line Number] => 73 )
)
```

So now we have an easy way of getting the results.

Along with simply comparing values (does `floor(1.56)` equal 1?) the class can also test for data types (is_string, is_bool, is_true, etc.—a full list is in the online User Guide.) You replace your:

```
$expected_result = 1;
```

line with something like:

```
$expected_result = 'is_float';
```

and the test proceeds as before.

If you've scattered these things throughout your code, it may run slowly, and will display all sorts of diagnostics on your screen. But you can stop this. Simply add the following line in your constructor:

```
$this->unit->active(FALSE);
```

And (surprise, surprise) if you change FALSE to TRUE, back it comes again. You can even do this dynamically.

When to Use Unit Tests

There is little point in testing whether a standard PHP function works. True. But there is value in testing your own functions to see if they consistently return the expected result. The main worry is always that:

- They will behave perfectly when you test them
- But a user will immediately think of a combination of circumstances you had never imagined, which will cause the function to fail
- Or you will write some more code, or alter existing code, and your own functions will no longer work properly

Sometimes, the failure is due to a programming issue, which can be caught by a unit test. You can have fun thinking up different parameters to test for.

Let's go back to our example of a function that performs a database query to delete a record with a given ID from a given table. What does it do if:

- The ID is NULL, or '', or not set? (Particularly important this one, as you might accidentally delete every entry in the table.)
- The ID is not an integer? ("x", for example?)
- The ID is an integer, but is out of range (you have 1000 entries in your table, but this ID is 1001?)
- The ID is a negative number?

and so on. It's quite amusing thinking of different conditions to test for.

Throw them all at the function with a unit test, and see. However, think carefully about the results you expect. The first case and second case are clearly programming errors. You should rewrite your program to prevent this happening. So if it does, you want the test to return failure.

We define the result we want from each test, so that we test if the program acted correctly, not if the parameter is correct. If we submit an 'x', that's an incorrect parameter; but if the program throws an exception, that is correct behavior. It helps to write all the tests to show 'passed' if the program is doing what we want, so we only have to take notice of exceptions.

The third case above, where the ID is an integer but out of range, is not necessarily a programming error. The database should be able to sort this out safely. However, what you need to do depends on your program and its objectives. Maybe, before you submit the integer value, you need to check that it is within range? Or maybe you are happy to let it run, in which case, because the program may return a database error message to your screen, you need to intercept this and replace it with a bland 'sorry, unable to do this at this time' error message? Or maybe test the delete operation for success and branch accordingly?

Example of a Unit Test

Let's build some code to test the 'delete' function. I've set up a 'delete' function (which is in a model) so that it detects that I am testing it, and on failure returns a value ($dbvalue).

```
if($test == 'yes')
    {
    $place =  __FILE__ . __LINE__ ;
```

```
$dbvalue = "exception at $place: sent state value $state to
                                   trydelete function ";
return $dbvalue;
}
```

If the test is successful, a similar loop returns a $dbvalue of 'OK'. The test code is simple. First, we build an array of ID values and the results we expect from each. In other words, if we try to delete using an ID of '' or 'abc' the system should throw an exception, prefixing the diagnostic line it returns with the word 'exception'. If it is 1, or 9999, the system should accept it as a valid ID, and prefix the line it returns with 'OK'.

So the array key is the condition you are testing for and the array value is the result you expect the function to return.

```
$numbers = array(
                ''          =>      'exception',
                'NULL'      =>      'exception',
                'x'         =>      'exception',
                '9999'      =>      'OK',
                '-1'        =>      'exception',
                '1'         =>      'OK'
                );
```

Now use the following code to loop through the $numbers array and use the CI unit test to do each test.

The test is to run the $this->delete() function, specifying the table you are deleting from ('fred') and the ID value ($testkey).

```
foreach($numbers AS $testkey => $testvalue)
{$dbvalue = $this->delete('fred', $testkey);
$result .= $this->unit->run(preg_match("/$testvalue/",
        $dbvalue), 1, $dbvalue);
    }
```

Remember, the CI unit test allows you to provide three parameters:

- $test: for each array key, we try the database by calling the delete function with $testkey, the array key—which is the ID (or lack of an ID) we are submitting to the function. The function returns a value (here called $dbvalue). Our $test is to compare that value, using a regex, to what we expect it to be—which is $testvalue, the value of the array. (Does it include 'OK' or 'exception'?)

- $expectedresult is '1', because if our code is correct we expect the regex to find a match. We expect 'NULL' to throw an exception and 1 to be OK.

- $testname: this parameter is optional: it is the string returned by the test, which goes on to explain what value we tried to use and what we were testing.

Here's the result, as shown in CI's inbuilt HTML format: All return the **Result** 'passed', so we can have confidence in our code. (The **Test Datatype** and **Expected Datatype** are always shown as integers, even though our inputs may not be integers, because the test is actually a regex comparison, which returns a 1 or a 0).

Test Name	exception at: E:\xampplite\htdocs\packt2\system\application\models\crud.php478 : id no of NULL set for delete op in fred, expecting integer
Test Datatype	Integer
Expected Datatype	Integer
Result	Passed
File Name	E:\xampplite\htdocs\packt2\system\application\models\crud.php
Line Number	615

Test Name	exception at: E:\xampplite\htdocs\packt2\system\application\models\crud.php478 : id no of x set for delete op in fred, expecting integer
Test Datatype	Integer
Expected Datatype	Integer
Result	Passed
File Name	E:\xampplite\htdocs\packt2\system\application\models\crud.php
Line Number	615

Test Name	OK at E:\xampplite\htdocs\packt2\system\application\models\crud.php441 : doing delete on id of 9999
Test Datatype	Integer
Expected Datatype	Integer
Result	Passed
File Name	E:\xampplite\htdocs\packt2\system\application\models\crud.php
Line Number	615

Test Name	exception at: E:\xampplite\htdocs\packt2\system\application\models\crud.php478 : id no of -1 set for delete op in fred, expecting integer
Test Datatype	Integer
Expected Datatype	Integer
Result	Passed
File Name	E:\xampplite\htdocs\packt2\system\application\models\crud.php

The fun, and actually quite useful, thing is thinking of new tests to include in the array!

For instance, what if the 'id' is a number, but not an integer? To try this with the above code, you'd add

```
'3.5'          =>        'exception',
```

to the array of test values.

However, you'd be surprised (as I was) to find that this test fails—in other words, it suggests that your function would accept 3.5 as an integer. The reason is that PHP does a 'loose' equality test; it finds a number and takes this for an integer. What you need in this case is a 'strict' mode of test that compares the datatype as well as the values. To set this, use:

```
$this->unit->use_strict(TRUE);
```

CI's Benchmarking Class

This class allows you to measure the time it takes for your program to go from one point to another. You insert one line of code to define the first point:

```
$this->benchmark->mark('here');
```

and another line of code to define the second:

```
$this->benchmark->mark('there');
```

then you insert a third line to tell you the elapsed time:

```
$fred =  $this->benchmark->elapsed_time('here', 'there');
```

You can then print the result, $fred, or do whatever else you want to do with it.

Benchmarks can have any name you like, as long as they are different, and you can have as many pairs as you want. You can use these tests to see if a particular part of your code is taking a suspiciously long time. If one of your pages takes too long to load, you can insert several benchmarks to identify the actual piece of code that is causing the delay.

For the tests in our website monitoring application, however, we aren't so much interested in one-off times. By the time we get our applications up on the Internet, we hope that their speed is acceptable. Absolute differences between times are likely to be small and largely meaningless. However, if we track a benchmark on several successive tests, we may notice that it is changing: and this may give us a clue to some underlying problem. A database query may be taking longer; or our hosting may be less effective. So for our purposes, we'll take the contents of $fred, and store it in our database.

CI's Profiler Class

The profiler class is simply brilliant. You put one line of code somewhere inside a function in your class. (It works from inside the constructor, so it makes sense to put it there.) That line is:

```
$this->output->enable_profiler(TRUE);
```

If you change your mind, either delete it or change it to:

```
$this->output->enable_profiler(FALSE);
```

In exchange for this one line of code, you get a full report on your screen, giving you details of the time CI took to load itself and your controller, of what was in the POST array, and of any database queries you have run. At the code development stage, this is a real help.

If you add in your own benchmarks, it will display those as well. You have to use special names for your benchmarks—they must end in _start and _end, respectively, and each pair must otherwise have the same name:

```
$this->benchmark->mark('fred_start');
```

and, somewhere else,

```
$this->benchmark->mark('fred_end');
```

You are now logged out. Goodbye!

Username: [   ]
Password: [   ]
         [Submit!]

0

BENCHMARKS

Loading Time Base Classes	0.2237
Fred	0.0054
Controller Execution Time (Start / Logout)	0.6031
Total Execution Time	0.8274

POST DATA

No POST data exists

QUERIES

INSERT INTO ci_sessions (session_id, ip_address, user_agent, last_activity) VALUES ('bfc406ba0eb660944f6d663b17dccaab', '127.0.0.1', 'Mozilla/5.0 (Windows; U, Windows NT 5.0, en-GB, rv', 1166196526)

UPDATE ci_sessions SET session_id = '' WHERE session_id = 'bfc406ba0eb660944f6d663b17dccaab'

As you can see, the time elapsed between these two benchmarks is then displayed as 'fred'.

Testing with Mock Databases

Dynamic sites are all about databases. If you are testing them properly, you ought to test whether your code can actually modify a database. End-to-end tests do this: for instance, if your test is whether you can log in with the correct username/password combination, you are probably reading a database to do so.

But testing whether you can update, create, and delete entries on a production database is a dangerous pastime, because it corrupts your real data!

Remember that CI allows you to declare more than one database, and to swap between them easily?—see Chapter 4. Using this, it's easy to set up a mock database, and then add, change, and delete data in it.

You can also use CI to set up and knock down tables, or possibly even whole databases depending on your host and your permission level. CI's:

```
$this->db->query('YOUR QUERY HERE');
```

function allows you to run any SQL query, including something like this:

```
$this->db->query('CREATE TABLE fred(id INT, name VARCHAR(12),
INDEX(id))');
```

which will create a new table, or something like this:

```
$this->db->query("INSERT INTO fred VALUES (1, 'smith')");
```

which will populate that table with one row of data.

So, with a few lines of code, CI lets you set up a whole new set of mock data to test, play around with it, test the results, and then delete it ready for next time. You might then run a set of unit tests on the delete() function to see if the function does what we expect when it has different 'id' parameters, as described earlier in this chapter.

Now you're going beyond the simple unit test. If we run a test that should have deleted the value in our table, then we need to check whether it actually has been deleted. This is easily done with the following code, again using CI's unit testing class, and its active record class:

```
$test        = $this->db->count_all('fred');
$expected_result = 0;
$test_name = 'tests number of entries left in table after unique
                                          entry removed';
$this->unit->run($test, $expected_result, $test_name);
```

`$this->db->count_all` counts all the results in the table, and we know that there should now be no results there at all. You can just as easily use this sort of code to check an 'insert' operation, to see if there is one more record in the table afterwards.

Because this is dummy data, which we created specially for the test, we know exactly what to expect, and it doesn't matter what we do to it. Just remember to destroy and rebuild the table between tests, otherwise you may get odd results.

Control and Timing

Testing is the heart of our application, so here's just a word about how it can be controlled.

You'll see from the database specification at the end of Chapter 4 that our application has a table called `tests`, and a table called `events`. Each time the site is asked to do a test run, it goes through the `tests` table, looking for two fields: `frequency` and `last_done`. If the `frequency` is, say, hourly, it checks the `last_done` field to see if the test has been done within an hour of the current time. If not, it does the test now, and updates its own `last_done` field to the current time.

When the test is done, however, the program creates an entry in the `events` table. This gives the ID of the site, and various other bits of information, most notably the result of the test. This table then provides the statistics we can use to build reports for ourselves or for clients, sorting out individual tests, or all tests on a given site, etc.

As a reminder of the benchmarking class that we discussed earlier in this chapter: when you run a test from a function like the one we just discussed, it's a good idea to put in benchmarks so you know how long the test is taking. Save the time to the `events` table. There's a field in this table for `timetaken`: it's a float data type because we are dealing in fractions of seconds. While the time taken to run any single test may be of little interest, changes of pattern when the test is run many times over at intervals may be interesting: they can show you if the test is speeding up or slowing down. If, for instance, it takes appreciably longer to log in to your pages, this might be because your ISP is overloading the server; it might be because you are putting too much code on your pages; or it might be that your site is becoming too popular and you need more bandwidth.

Either way, testing regularly and presenting the aggregated results in a usable format can give you useful early warnings of problems.

Summary

We've spent a lot of time on testing. It's not the most exciting of subjects, but if you're writing websites that matter, it's a great way of making sure you sleep peacefully at night.

We've seen how CI normally handles errors, displaying them to you as you write code, but allowing you to turn them off (or divert them to a log file) when your site goes in to production mode.

We looked at unit tests and CI's tools for handling these. We also looked at benchmarking, a class which makes it simple you to monitor the execution time of different part of your program.

The profiler tool is great for showing you a lot of information about your code as you develop it. CI offers a good suite of tools for developing and testing your own code.

We also looked at ways of testing with dummy database tables, to see whether database operations have actually taken place as we expected.

We then integrated some external code with CI, to allow us to build web robots and therefore to run our own 'end-to-end' tests on a remote site.

9
Using CI to Communicate

The main strength of the Internet is its ability to communicate. This chapter looks at three ways in which CI makes communication easier.

First, we'll add to our testing toolkit by using CI's FTP class to access remote files directly.

Then, we'll use the email class to make our site automatically email us when certain conditions are met.

Lastly, we'll venture into Web 2.0 territory — using XML-RPC to create a private 'web service' that allows our remote sites to take action and return information on a request form our testing site.

Using the FTP Class to Test Remote Files

File Transfer Protocol (FTP) is a method of transferring files over the Internet. It's normally used to move files backwards and forwards to your website, using a special FTP program. It's something most of us only use occasionally, when we are putting up a new site.

You can, however, automate the whole process painlessly with CI. One use is to test the integrity of your remote site: are the files still there? As a website owner, you always face the possibility that someone will tamper with the files on your site. It may just be your ISP or your server admin, mistakenly deleting or over-writing something. (I had this happen to me once, when my ISP rebuilt their server and forgot to reload one of my application files. The file concerned wasn't used very often, but mattered a lot when it was. This led to an interesting error that took some time to track down!)

As one example of the power of the FTP class, let's build a regular test program, to check the files on a remote site. A few lines of code are all we need:

```
function getremotefiles($hostname, $username, $password)
    {
    $this->load->library('ftp');
    $config['hostname'] = $hostname;
    $config['username'] = $username;
    $config['password'] = $password;
    $config['debug']    = TRUE;
    $this->ftp->connect($config);
    $filelist = $this->ftp->list_files('/my_directory/');
    $this->ftp->close();
    return $list;
    }
```

First, load the FTP library if you haven't already done so. Then, define the configuration parameters: hostname (e.g., www.mysite.com), username, and password for your FTP access.

Once connected, CI's FTP class gives you several options. In this case, we've used list_files() to return a list of files in the /my_directory/ folder. The function returns an array, and you can easily check this against an array of the files that you expect to find there. As before, we're trying to list all our tests in a database. So this time we need to list the FTP URL (or host name), the user name and password, and instead of a regex, the array of files to check against. To maintain the integrity of this array, if you store it inside your database, you will need to serialize it before you put it in, and un-serialize it when you take it out again.

Then it's easy to compare the $remotearray returned by the getremotefiles() function with the un-serialized $referencearray returned by your database:

```
function comparefiles($remotearray, $referencearray)
    {
    $report = "<br />On site, not in reference array: ";
    $report .= print_r(array_diff($remotearray, $referencearray), TRUE);
    $report .= "<br />In reference array, not on site: ";
    $report .= print_r(array_diff($referencearray, $remotearray), TRUE);
    return $report;
    }
```

The PHP `array_diff` function compares the second array to the first, so it will list files present in the first, but not in the second. So, run the function twice, reversing the order of the array parameters: that way you get two lists, one of what isn't on your site (but should be) and one of what is on your site (but shouldn't be). The first should show any files that your ISP has accidentally deleted, the second any files that may have been added.

The CI FTP class also allows you to upload, move, rename, and delete files. Suppose that your test above reveals that one of the files in your reference array (let's call it `myfile.php` is missing from your site. You can use the FTP class to upload it:

```
$this->ftp->upload('c:/myfile.php', '/public_html/myfile.php');
```

In this example, the local path is given first, and the path on the remote server second. Optionally, you can specify in a third parameter how the file should be uploaded (as ASCII or binary.) If you don't, CI makes its own decision based on the file extension—which will usually be correct. If you are running PHP5, you can add a fourth parameter to set the file permissions, assuming you are uploading to a Linux server.

Be very careful about the delete option. As the user guide says, "It will recursively delete **everything** within the supplied path, including sub-folders and all files". Even writing this paragraph has made me nervous.

Using a combination of the FTP delete and upload functions, you could automatically update the files on your remote sites. List the files you need to update, and visit each site in turn, first deleting each old one, and then uploading each new one.

There is also an interesting 'mirror' function, which allows you to set up a complete duplicate of a website on another server.

If you are running PHP5, the FTP class also has a function that allows you to change file permissions.

As you can see, there's plenty of scope for expanding your application from testing your remote websites to actually maintaining or updating them. You could, for instance, write code to distribute updates automatically.

Machines Talking to Machines Again—XML-RPC

The Web 2.0 revolution is largely built on machine-to-machine interfaces, which allow mashups and APIs and all those good things.

This is the basis of 'web services'. You can offer an interface to your site that allows other people to use it to do something for them. To give a simple example, if you set up a 'web service' that converts temperatures in centigrade to Fahrenheit, the client sends in a request with one parameter (the temperature to be converted) and the server returns the converted value. So, anyone can add a temperature conversion function that appears to be on his or her own site, but is actually calling yours.

XML-RPC allows two machines to talk directly. The receiving site creates a simple API (application programming interface). Anyone who wants to talk to it needs to know that API—what methods are available, what parameters they take, and what the syntax is—for addressing them. Many major sites use this system: Google, for instance, allows you to make direct calls to its search engine or to Google Earth via a published API.

Setting up your own private API is relatively easy, thanks to CI. You need two websites to set this up and to test it, which makes it a little more complex than most things. One site (let's call it the 'receiving' site) is the one that offers the API, listens out for requests, and answers them. (In our example, this is one of the remote sites that we are trying to test and manage.) The other site makes the request using the API and gets the answer back. (In our example, this is the test site itself.)

In the XML-RPC protocol, the two sites talk by means of highly structured XML. (Hence the name XML-RPC—it's short for XML Remote Procedure Call.) The client sends an XML packet to the 'receiving site' server, stating the function it wants to use and any arguments or parameters to be passed. The server decodes the XML and, if it fits the API, calls the function and returns a response, also structured as XML, which the client decodes and acts on.

Your API consists of the functions that the receiving site offers, and instructions for how to use them—e.g., what parameters they take, what data type these should be, etc.

On the receiving site, we create an XML-RPC server, which makes the selected internal methods available to external sites. These 'internal methods' are actually just normal functions within one of your controllers: the server's role is to handle the interface between the external call and the internal function.

There are two sets of problems when you set up an XML-RPC process:

- Getting the two sites to talk to each other
- Making sure that the data is transmitted in a suitable format

Both rely heavily on multi-dimensional arrays, which machines can take in their stride, even if humans need to puzzle over them a bit. CI makes it a lot easier—though it's still quite tricky to get right.

Getting the XML-RPC Server and Client in Touch with Each Other

First, you have to set up a server on the remote site, and a client on the requesting site. This can be done with a few simple lines of code. Let's say we are doing the server in a controller called 'mycontroller' (on the receiving site) and the client in a controller called 'xmlrpc_client' (on the requesting site).

In each case, start off by initializing the CI classes within the constructor. There are two; for a client you only need to load the first, for a server you need to load them both:

```
$this->load->library('xmlrpc');
$this->load->library('xmlrpcs');
```

Now, for the server. Close your constructor function, and within the 'mycontroller' `index()` function, define the functions you are offering up to the outside world. You do this by building a 'functions' sub-array (within the main CI `$config` array) which maps the names of the incoming requests to the actual functions you want to use:

```
$config['functions']['call'] = array('function' => 'mycontroller.
myfunction');
$config['functions']['call2'] = array('function' => 'mycontroller.
myfunction2');
```

In this case, there are two named function calls — 'call' and 'call2'. This is what the request asks for. (It doesn't ask for the functions by name, but by the name of the call. Of course, you can use the same name if you wish.) For each call, you define a sub-sub-array giving the 'function' within the controller — i.e. 'myfunction' and 'myfunction2' respectively.

You then finish off your server by initializing it and instantiating it:

```
$this->xmlrpcs->initialize($config);
$this->xmlrpcs->serve();
```

and it is now ready to listen for requests.

Now you need to go to the other website — the client — and set up an XML-RPC client to make the requests. This should be a separate controller on your client site. It's quite short:

```
$server_url = 'http://www.mysite.com/index.php/mycontroller';
$this->load->library('xmlrpc');
$this->xmlrpc->set_debug(TRUE);
$this->xmlrpc->server($server_url, 80);
$this->xmlrpc->method('call');
```

You define the URL of the receiving site, specifying the controller that contains the XML-RPC server that you want. You load the XML-RPC class, define the server, and the method you want to use—this is the name of the call you want to make, not of the actual function you want to use. If the function you are calling needs parameters, you pass them this way:

```
$request = array('optimisation','sites');
```

As you see, we're passing two here.

Then, you check if a response has been received, and do something with it:

```
if ( ! $this->xmlrpc->send_request())
{
        echo $this->xmlrpc->display_error();
}
else
{
        print_r($this->xmlrpc->display_response());
}
```

The simplest option is to display it; but in a real application you're more likely to want the machine to analyze it, e.g., by using a regex, and then to act on the results. For instance, if the result contains an error message, you might want to record the error in your database, and take action to report it to the human user.

Formatting XML-RPC Exchanges

Let's use a real, if simplified, example. In this section, we will create an XML-RPC call/response that lets you remotely trigger a database optimization.

The client we wrote above, is asking for a method known as 'call' and supplying two parameters: 'optimisation' and 'sites'.

The server on the receiving site maps this request for 'call' onto a function called 'myfunction'.

Let's have a look at this function. It's basically an ordinary function within the controller. It attempts to optimize a MySQL database table, and returns 'success' or 'failure' depending on the result.

```
function myfunction($request)
{
 $parameters = $request->output_parameters();
 $function = $parameters['0'];
 $table =   $parameters['1'];
```

```
if ($this->db->query("OPTIMIZE TABLE $table"))
{
        $content = 'Success';
}
else
{
        $content = 'failure';
}
$response = array(
                array(
                'function'    => array($function, 'string'),
                'table'       => array($table, 'string'),
                'result'      => array($content, 'string'),
                        ),
                        'struct');
return $this->xmlrpc->send_response($response);
}
```

Note the `$request`, set as the function parameter. This contains the `$request` array from the client—remember, it had two values, 'optimisation' and 'sites'. CI has transformed the array into an object, `$request`. So you can't get the individual parameters by treating it as an array, instead you have to use the `$request ->output_parameters()` method of the `$request` object. This returns an array, which you interrogate in the normal way.

Using this, we have told the function on the receiving site which table we want to optimize, the 'sites' table. We've also told it what to call the function ('optimisation'). It adds a further parameter called 'result', gets the value, and returns all three to us.

The result it sends back to the client site looks something like this:

```
<?xml version="1.0" encoding="UTF-8"?>
<methodResponse>
 <params>
  <param>
   <value>
    <struct>
     <member>
       <name>function</name>
        <value>
         <string>optimisation</string>
        </value>
     </member>
     <member>
      <name>table</name>
```

```
          <value>
            <string>sites</string>
          </value>
        </member>
        <member>
          <name>result</name>
          <value>
            <string>Success</string>
          </value>
        </member>
        </struct>
      </value>
    </param>
  </params>
</methodResponse>
```

(Except it's not indented: I did that to make the structure clearer.)

As you can see, our simple three word response (optimisation, exercises, success) has been wrapped in verbose layers of tags, in a way sadly typical of XML, to tell a machine exactly what is going on. There are three `<member></member>` tag pairs. Each has a `<name></name>` pair ('function', 'table', 'result' respectively). And each of these has a `<value></value>` pair, which includes (as well as the data type) the actual information we want—i.e. 'optimisation','sites','success'.

Never mind that I don't like it. Computers thrive on this sort of stuff: it is precise, unambiguous, and easy for a machine to read. This chapter is about computers talking to each other, not about user-friendly interfaces.

Now, your XML-RPC client function on your calling site can extract the values it wants and act on them. It's easy to do this with a regex, because each answer is clearly demarcated by XML mark-up brackets.

Note how CI spares you a lot of fiddling around with angle brackets—you didn't need to write any of this stuff.

Debugging

As soon as you start to test your client/sever combination, you will probably get this message:

```
The XML data received was either invalid or not in the correct form
for XML-RPC. Turn on debugging to examine the XML data further.
```

Turn on debugging, by including the line:

```
$this->xmlrpc->set_debug(TRUE);
```

in your client. This allows you to see exactly what your client-receiving site combination is sending back to you. Be warned, this is where debugging gets quite frustrating.

There are several places where the exchange can go wrong:

- The remote site is not responding properly. (You may have to temporarily set it to display errors in order to work out why it is not responding. This is annoying if it is an active site. The additional Catch 22 is that it will then display—i.e. return as HTML—error messages, which aren't part of the XML response your client expects, so you will get a second set of error messages, caused by the first set...) Debugging this may involve quite a lot of FTP transfers back and forth, until you get it right.

- The client code may not be working properly.

- You have got the URL wrong. (This needs to be CI's way of addressing the controller in which the XML_RPC server sits—i.e. `http://www.mysite.com/ index.php/mycontroller`. If you put all the server code in the controller constructor instead of in the index function, it will still work, but you need to address the function you want to call by name—e.g. `http://www.mysite.com/ index.php/mycontroller/myfunction`).

- The XML interchange may not be exactly right. The `set_debug` function allows you to see what is being sent back, but you can spend quite a while staring at this trying to work out where it has gone wrong. (Believe me...)

However, once you get all this right, you've done something quite clever. You've built a function in a remote site, and called it remotely.

In other words, you've set up an application that can do maintenance or other operations on remote sites. If you have several remote sites to manage, you can easily replicate this across them, allowing you (for instance) to optimize all your database tables once a day by one action on just one site.

Issues with XML-RPC?

Security is an issue, of course. You would want to password-protect your function calls, so that the client had to send a password as a parameter before the receiving site responded. This can be done simply by sending the password as an additional parameter in the request, and having the called function check it before responding.

If you were exposing critical functions, you might want the whole thing to take place behind an SSL layer. Our example looks harmless—you might not mind if a hacker repeatedly broke in to your site, but all he or she did was tidy up your database for you each time. On the other hand, it would be a good basis for a Denial of Service attack.

It has to be said that XML-RPC is frustrating and time-consuming to set up and debug, even with CI's very considerable help. You are writing and debugging two sites at once, and the XML format for transmitting data between them can only be called picky. It doesn't let you get away with even the smallest mistake.

Some would argue that XML-RPC is a superseded technology, with most new interfaces or APIs being written in more complex languages such as SOAP (which are even more time-consuming to set up) .

However, for our purposes, XML-RPC is ideal. It allows us to make our remote websites perform complex internal functions without bothering us with the details.

Talking to Humans for a Change: the Email Class

We've put together a lot of the building blocks for our web test site. We have a database of tests, and we've built functions to run different types of tests. We can access our site and check that we are seeing the right page; we can check that all the files are where we expect them to be on the remote server. We can automatically run functions on the site and get it to optimize itself. It's fairly simple to write code that uses these tools to run a suite of tests whenever we want, either when we log on or by some automatic reminder, such as setting a 'cron' job on a Linux server to start our program running at suitable intervals.

But it's not really enough to run tests and just store the results away in a database. If something is wrong, we need to know as soon as possible.

Here's where CI's email class comes in. It allows us to program our site to send us emails whenever certain conditions are reached. You might want to send an email for each failed test, or you might want to run a series of tests, collect the results, and then send just one email report.

To use the email class, first (as always) you have to load it.

```
$this->load->library('email');
```

Then we have to set some configuration variables. This is where we can run into problems, because the class depends on the server that is hosting our code being able (and willing) to send email for us. Once again, we may have to check with the ISP. (It's also difficult to test this on a local site, because Xampplite, for instance, may not be able to offer you a mail server.)

However, once we've sorted out your ISP, we can easily configure the email class. There are a lot of options, all listed in the on-line user guide. The main ones are:

- protocol: does your system use mail, sendmail or SMTP to send emails?
- mailpath: where is your system's mail program stored?

You set them like this:

```
$config['protocol'] = 'sendmail';
$config['mailpath'] = '/usr/sbin/sendmail';
$this->email->initialize($config);
```

Other options, all of which have sensible defaults, include things like word-wrapping, character sets, whether you want to send text or HTML emails, and so on. Setting the options up and getting them working is the only (potentially) difficult part of using this class.

Once you've loaded the class and initialized it, using it is ridiculously intuitive.

```
$this->email->from('david@mysite.com');
$this->email->to('someone@myownsite.com');
$this->email->bcc('fred@somewhere.com');
$this->email->subject('Test message');
$this->email->message('Hello world');
$this->email->send();
```

will send me an email, copied to my client, reporting whatever message I want.

If you're sending more than one email, start each new one with:

```
$this->email->clear()
```

just to make sure that you start with a clean slate each time.

You can also use the email class to send attachments. Remember that the attachment file must already be saved on the server that is sending the email, and you have to specify where, in terms of the server root file (giving the server address, not the web address).

Get its address and name like this:

```
$path = $this->config->item('server_root');
$file = $path.'/my_subdirectory/myfile.htm';
```

then just add this line:

```
$this->email->attach($file);
```

before the `$this->email->send();`.

This simple CI function is so much easier than trying to write out the full PHP code to send attachments. It handles all the protocols involved, without you even having to be aware of them.

If you include the line:

```
$result = $this->email->print_debugger();
```

in your code, and print out the `$result` variable, you'll get a screenful of useful information, like this:

```
Your message has been successfully sent using the following protocol:
mail
User-Agent: Code Igniter
Date: Wed, 18 Apr 2007 13:50:41 +0100
From:
Return-Path:
Bcc: fred@somewhere.com
Reply-To: "david@mysite.com"
X-Sender: david@mysie.com
X-Mailer: Code Igniter
X-Priority: 3 (Normal)
Message-ID: <462614219c1a6@upton.cc>
Mime-Version: 1.0
Content-Type: multipart/mixed; boundary="B_ATC_462614219d14d"
This is a multi-part message in MIME format.
Your email application may not support this format.

--B_ATC_462614219d14d
Content-Type: text/plain; charset=utf-8
Content-Transfer-Encoding: 8bit
test message
hello world

--B_ATC_462614219d14d
Content-type: text/html; name="myfile.html"
Content-Disposition: attachment;
Content-Transfer-Encoding: base64
```

(etc. etc.)

If something went wrong, then the debug information will return any server error messages as well. For instance, if I set the delivery method to SMTP without setting the right host or permissions:

```
$config['protocol'] = 'smtp';
```

it can't send the message, and it tells me:

```
You did not specify a SMTP hostname
Unable to send email using PHP SMTP. Your server might not be
configured to send mail using this method.
```

Bear in mind, however, that 'sendmail' is potentially misleading here—it returns a success message if it has passed the message on within the server, but this doesn't necessarily mean that the message has actually been sent. (So if you set the wrong 'mailpath' option, 'sendmail' may report that it has sent the email, when it actually hasn't.) CI relies on the messages it gets back from the mail sending application, so it can be fooled. As always with emails, they only way to be sure they have gone is to check that they've arrived—but that's another story.

CI's email class includes several useful options, all explained in the online User Guide. For instance, you can set it to send text or HTML format mail—if you chose HTML there's even a function to allow you to set a separate 'text' message for people who don't accept HTML email.

You can also set it to use different character sets, and to handle word-wrapping. You can set batch sizes, if you intend to send a lot of emails to a long mailing list, so that your server doesn't get overloaded. (Or your ISP doesn't panic and shut you down, thinking you are a spammer.)

Summary

We've now used CI to build some very sophisticated tools for our website, which give it some significant functionality.

Firstly, we used CI's FTP class to simplify and automate file transfer operations. Initially, we've just used this class to check that the files we expect to find on our site are actually there, and that noting unexpected has been added. This in itself is a valuable check, as many of the problems websites throw at you involve unexpected alterations of files, usually by site admins but sometimes by hackers. This function will check regularly. The CI FTP class also offers the possibility of remote maintenance and updating of sites.

Then we looked at developing our own private 'web services' using CI's XML-RPC classes. These allow us automatically to call functions on a remote site, pass in parameters if necessary, and have the results returned to us—just as if we'd been logged on to the remote site instead of to our test site. We used this to have the remote site optimize a table in its database, and report back to us. Once again, we've gone beyond our original plan of simply monitoring the remote sites. Now we are able to instruct them to check or optimize themselves as well.

Lastly, we looked at the CI email class, which allows our testing site to generate emails. The CI code is extremely simple to use, and means that our site can notify us whenever it thinks there is a problem. CI makes it simple to build and send an email, and even to send attachments.

10
How CI Helps to Provide Dynamic Information

We've put a lot of thought into building our test website now, and CI has made it easy to do some very complex things. We've set up databases, used FTP, built tests, and started to email the test results. But it's easy to get caught up in techie things and forget that websites are often judged largely on presentation, on how well they process data, and how appropriately they display it to human users.

Here are a few CI classes that help with some problems that arise regularly when you are building a website, particularly when it comes to delivering dynamic information to your users:

- The date helper translates different date formats and helps you cope with time zones.

- The text and inflector helpers provide useful functions to manipulate and convert strings.

- The language class makes it easier to write websites that display the same information in different languages, depending on user preference.

- The table class—saves a lot of tedious `<tr><td>`s.

- You can automatically cache high-load dynamic pages for a faster response.

Each of these can save you a lot of coding time, while making your site look more professional (and keeping it easier to update).

The Date Helper: Converting and Localizing Dates

You know those websites that expect you to understand machine dates? MySQL's native 'timestamp' format, for example, is very useful, but it looks very careless to let your site users see things like:

```
20070124161830
```

or even:

```
2007-01-24 16:18:30
```

Of course, most people can work out what it means, but it gives your site an unprofessional and unfinished air. CI comes to the rescue with its date helper. This is loaded with:

```
$this->load->helper('date');
```

and immediately gives you access to a lot of useful functions. See the online User Guide for a full description.

Dates can be specified in many different ways. CI's `standard_date()` function gives you ten ways of displaying the same date:

1: atom	2006-12-31T11:34:44Q
2: cookie	Sunday, 31-Dec-06 11:34:44 UTC
3: iso	2006-12-31T11:34:44+0000
4: RFC 822	Sun, 31 Dec 06 11:34:44 +0000
5: RFC 850	Sunday, 31-Dec-06 11:12:34 UTC
6: RFC 1036	Sun, 31 Dec 06 11:34:44 +0000
7: RFC 1123	Sun, 31 Dec 2006 11:34:44 +0000
8: RFC 2822	Sun, 31 Dec 2006 11:34:44 +0000
9: RSS	Sun, 31 Dec 2006 11:34:44 +0000
10: W3C	2006-12-31T11:34:44Q

All you need to do is specify which you want. For instance:

```
$time = now();
echo standard_date('DATE_RFC822', $time);
```

There are also functions to convert between different types of date/time values. Their names are self-explanatory, and the exact syntax is described in the online User Guide. They enable you to do quite clever conversions very simply.

For instance, this code:

```
function converttimes()
{
$this->load->helper('date');
$mysql     = '20070101120000';
$table     = '';
$table .= "<table><tr><td width='50%'>Start with MySQL
time<td>$mysql</td></tr>";
$utime     = mysql_to_unix($mysql);
$table .= "<tr><td>now convert to unix timestamp<td>$utime</td></tr>";

$htime = unix_to_human($utime);
$table .= "</td></tr><tr><td>then back to 'human' time<td>$htime</
td></tr>";

$ttime = gmt_to_local($utime, 'UP25');
$table .= "</td></tr><tr><td>now convert unix stamp to local time in
Tehran<td>$ttime</td></tr>";

$ltime = unix_to_human($ttime);
$table .= "</td></tr><tr><td>and say that in human time <td>$ltime</
td></tr>";
$table .= "<table>";
echo $table;
}
```

produces this result:

Start with MySQL time	20070101120000
now convert to unix timestamp	1167652800
then back to 'human' time	2007-01-01 12:00 PM
now convert unix stamp to local time in Tehran	1167661800
and say that in human time	2007-01-01 02:30 PM

There's a lot of useful code available to you behind these functions, and they make international time zones, in particular, much easier to use.

The date helper also has `timezone_menu()`, a function that generates a drop-down menu of time zones. You can use this in conjunction with a database to allow site users to select a time zone, and later to present all their time references in their own 'local' time. In exchange for writing:

```
echo timezone_menu();
```

you get the following screenshot:

It looks at first as if CI offers an automatic way to handle time zones too, in the date helper's now() function. The User Guide suggests that you set the 'master time reference' in your config file to 'local' or 'gmt', using:

```
$config['time_reference'] = 'local';
```

Local is the default. If you set it to 'gmt', the code appears to return the system time (if there is one) based on the PHP mktime() function; if this is not valid, or you set the config file to 'local', it returns a time based on the time() function.

However, both of these are dependent on your server: it must be set to an accurate time and its default time zone must be set. (You can check this with phpinfo().) But the time zone may not be set, and your server may not be in the same time zone as you: this is quite common with large companies, for example.

So CI itself doesn't actually know what your time zone offset is, though it may be able to get your server's offset. Therefore, if you used timezone_menu() to capture users' time zone preferences, you can't just rely on the date helper's now() function to translate GMT times to their local times. You will need to look up their preferences, and write separate code to translate times whenever you want to display them.

Working with Text: the Text Helper and Inflector Helper

The text helper has a series of functions that help you to manipulate text in various ways. See the online User Guide for full details. I'd just like to show you a few of the useful things you can do.

The `word_limiter()` function intelligently truncates strings to a length you set. `word_wrap()` wraps text to a length you specify. And `word_censor()` replaces words you don't want to see with harmless equivalents.

There are also functions to convert `ascii_to_entities()` and back again, which may help prevent those times when text in formats like MS Word displays oddly if you copy it to a web page.

Inflector helper functions will change words from singular to plural or vice versa, though they are caught out by irregular forms like 'sheep/sheep' and 'child/ children', and would make some mistakes, e.g., turning 'day' into 'daies'. They can also 'camelize', or underscore spaces between multiple words, and then turn them back again.

You can have fun with these, for instance, this code:

```
function converttext()
    {
    $this->load->helper('text');
    $this->load->helper('inflector');
    $mytext = "Mr Bill Gates is a man I like. He is a very clever man
       and writes superb software";
    echo "$mytext<br />";
    $disallowed = array('like', 'clever', 'superb');
    $string = word_censor($mytext, $disallowed);
    echo "Censored, this might read: ";
    echo "$string<br />";
    $mywtext = word_limiter($mytext, 3);
    $mytext = underscore($mywtext);
    echo " His name could be written like this $mytext";
    $mytext = camelize($mywtext);
    echo "or like this $mytext";
    }
```

will give you this result:

Mr Bill Gates is a man I like. He is a very clever man and writes superb software
Censored, this might read: Mr Bill Gates is a man I ####. He is a very ######
man and writes ###### software
His name could be written like this mr_bill_gates...or like this mrBillGates...

These functions can be extremely useful if you are taking in text from other sources and need to convert it in one way or another, or to censor it. They may save you a lot of time spent writing regexes.

Going International: the Language Class

If you are writing a website that may be viewed in more than one country, CI can present pages in more than one language for you. It works like this:

Firstly, you identify the text presented to your users that needs to be translated. Let's go back to one of the first examples of displaying dynamic data that we discussed in this book. Your welcome page might be called by code in a model, which says:

```
function hello($name)
{
        $data['mytitle'] =    'Welcome to this site';
        $data['mytext'] =     "Hello, $name, now we're getting
                                                   dynamic!";
        $this->load->view('testview', $data);
}
```

The strings assigned to the $data array are the messages displayed to the user:

But you might know that the user was a German speaker—perhaps because of the location of his or her server, or possibly because he or she was logged in, and had stated a language preference. It would be nice if you could greet him or her in German. CI provides an easy method to do this.

First, you need to set up a language file. If you look in the system folder, you'll see there already is a language folder with an English sub-folder. This in turn contains a series of files—e.g., unit_test_lang.php. This is a PHP file that simply defines an associative array of expressions to be shown to users:

```php
<?php
$lang['ut_test_name']          = 'Test Name';
$lang['ut_test_datatype']      = 'Test Datatype ';
$lang['ut_res_datatype']       = 'Expected Datatype';
$lang['ut_result']             = 'Result';

// etc etc///
?>
```

The array values are the expressions you want displayed, the array keys are whatever shorthand you want to use to identify them to yourself. The filename must end with '_lang'.

We need to set up our own, in each of the languages we want to show. Let's call the first one welcome_lang.php and save it in the system/language/English sub-folder. It should look like this:

```php
<?php
$lang['welcome_title']         = 'Welcome to this site';
$lang['welcome_text1']         = 'Hello ';
$lang['welcome_text2']         = ' now we're getting dynamic';
?>
```

The array keys can be anything you like: but it's a good idea to prefix them, say with 'ut' for the unit test language array, and 'welcome' for the array we're writing now. They all go into the same base array, so if you inadvertently enter two values with identical keys, the second will overwrite the first.

The original function that set up the page needs to be altered. Firstly, you need to load the language file. In this example, I've included it in the function, but normally, it makes more sense to do it inside the class constructor. Notice that although the file name ends in _lang (welcome_lang.php), you omit this suffix when you load it (i.e. you load 'welcome', not 'welcome_lang'). Secondly, you use the array keys instead of actual text—that is, to say:

```php
function hello($name)
{
        $this->lang->load('welcome');

        $data['mytitle']=    $this->lang->line('welcome_title');
        $data['mytext']=     $this->lang->line('welcome_text1');
        $data['mytext'].=    $name;
```

```
                        $data['mytext'].=     $this->lang->line('welcome_text2');
                        $this->load->view('testview', $data);

        }
```

But this only gives us the same page as we had before: it's still in English. If we want to allow translation into German, we need another language file. Firstly, we create a new subfolder: alongside `system/language/english` we create `system/language/german`. In the new folder, we save a file with exactly the same name as the English version: 'welcome_lang.php'. (Not willkommen_sprach.php—sorry, just my little joke.)

This file is identical to the English original—on the left-hand side of the array, at least. The keys are the same, but the array values on the right-hand side now have to be in German.

```php
<?php
$lang['welcome_title']        = 'Willkommen auf dieser Web Seite';
$lang['welcome_text1']        = 'Guten tag ';
$lang['welcome_text2']        = 'jetzt sind wir dynamisch!';
?>
```

(I'm afraid that you have to do the translation yourself—CI doesn't do that for you!)

There's one thing left to do. When the original 'hello' function loaded the language file:

```
$this->lang->load('welcome_lang');
```

it did not specify which language, so the default was English. As you might expect, the default language is specified in the 'config' file:

```
$config['language']     = "english";
```

To get German, the language loading expression in the 'hello' function should additionally specify the name of the folder in which the German array is saved. (Logically enough, this is 'german'.)

So the function now says:

```
function hello($name)
{
        $this->lang->load('welcome', 'german');

        $data['mytitle']=   $this->lang->line('welcome_title');
        $data['mytext']=    $this->lang->line('welcome_text1);
        $data['mytext'].=   $fred;
        $data['mytext'].=   $this->lang->line('welcome_text2);

        $this->load->view('testview', $data);
}
```

and the resulting page looks like this:

All we need to do now is to ensure that our function loads the right language dynamically.

Assuming we've detected the user's language preference, and stored it in the variable `$user_language_pref`, we need something to load the language files conditionally, like this:

```
if($user_language_pref == 'german')
    {$this->lang->load('welcome', 'german');}
elseif($user_language_pref == 'french')
    {$this->lang->load('welcome', 'french');}
// etc etc
```

It takes a degree of self-discipline to write a code like this. You have to remember never to put actual text into your code, but instead to create an entry in a language file each time. But once you've done that, all you have to do is copy the language file and give it to someone to translate into your target language(s), and your site is magically available in translation. If you change the wording of the site, you only have to change the language files. If you have used some expressions more than once, you don't have to hunt through the pages looking for each example.

If your site uses long stretches of complex text, it becomes less viable to translate it in this way. But for the 'boilerplate' text scattered around every website, CI's language class works well and makes your site look much more impressive.

Making HTML Tables the Easy Way: the Table Class

I've been using CI for some months now, but I keep stumbling on functions that make life easier.

Here's a good example, for anyone who spends a lot of time writing things like:

```
echo "<tr><td>$value1</td><td>$value2</td></tr>";
```

CI's table class allows you to auto-generate HTML tables. Let's display details of some of the tests we've run. You start off by loading the class, as always. Then you can specify the table data as an array, like this:

```
$this->load->library('table');
$data = array(
            array('name', 'type', 'time'),
            array('test 1', 'ping', '1166627335'),
            array('test 2', 'ping', '1166627335'),
            array('test 3', 'ete', '1166702400')
            );
echo $this->table->generate($data);
```

But the function really comes into its own when you automatically generate the data directly from the object returned by a database query. For instance, this short piece of code:

```
function dotable()
{
   $this->load->database();
   $this->load->library('table');
   $query = $this->db->query("SELECT name,type,time FROM events");
   echo $this->table->generate($query);
}
```

gives you the query results in a properly formatted HTML table. I can't resist showing it, though the default format is dull!

name	type	time
not set	test	1166627335
not set	test	1166627882
not set	test	1166628621
not set		1166700269
ete	test	1166700394
ete	test	1166700928
ete	test	1166701193
ete	test	1166702238
ete	test	1166702361
ete	test	1166702400
ete	test	1166703348
ete	test	1166703451
ete	test	1166703835
ete	test	1166703851
ete	test	1166703928
ete	test	1166704104
ete	test	1166712129
ete	test	1166712176
ete	test	1166712209

That's an amazing saving of your time—just four lines of code returns a query and wraps it up for you in HTML. In fact, a small tear comes to my eye when I think of all the time I used to spend writing:

```
<table>
<tr><td>$variable1</td><td>$variable2</td></tr> //etc.
```

While, as you can see, CI's basic table layout isn't wonderful, you can set your own template, using CSS styles if you wish, and the function will faithfully follow that. The template is an array inside the 'table' class, so you will need to reset it each time you call the class.

```
$tmpl = array (
                    'table_open'            => '<table border="0" cellpadding="4" cellspacing="0">',

                    'heading_row_start'     => '<tr>',
                    'heading_row_end'       => '</tr>',
                    'heading_cell_start'    => '<th>',
                    'heading_cell_end'      => '</th>',

                    'row_start'             => '<tr>',
```

```
                        'row_end'               => '</tr>',
                        'cell_start'            => '<td>',
                        'cell_end'              => '</td>',

                        'row_alt_start'         => '<tr>',
                        'row_alt_end'           => '</tr>',
                        'cell_alt_start'        => '<td>',
                        'cell_alt_end'          => '</td>',

                        'table_close'           => '</table>'
        );
```

```
    $this->table->set_template($tmpl);
```

There is a default template array, which looks like this, on which the function bases its design. Note that there are two sets of row definitions (row and row_alt), in case you want the colors of the rows to alternate.

If you submit revisions to part or all of the template, the function reacts accordingly, generating different HTML markup.

You'll have noticed that the template is just an array, and you submit revisions by revising the values for each key. For instance, if you have a CSS file defined somewhere with a class called mytable, you can refer to that:

```
    $tmpl = array ( 'table_open'  => '<table class="mytable">' );
```

You don't have to alter every value: those you don't alter remain at the default setting.

Now your table magically jumps out in the format you specified.

Caching Pages

By now, we're writing some pretty complex code. The server has to sit down and puzzle out each dynamically generated page. While it's simple for you to write a function like dotable() above, the poor old server has to do more work as a result.

Sometimes, this can lead to your pages taking longer to load than you would like. There may be no way round this. If you're writing a report that will be different each time you write it, then you just have to wait. However, you may be generating a page that will stay the same for a while. A blog, for instance, stays the same until you put another entry on it. If your blog gets a thousand views a day, on a day when you didn't add a new posting, each view will be the same, and it's a waste of time for the system to re-generate the same page over and over.

The way round this is to cache the page. You generate the page once, and the HTML produced is saved in a 'cache' file with a timestamp, as well as being returned to someone's browser for display on their screen. Then, when the next viewer requests that page, the system checks to see how long ago it was last generated and saved. If this is within a time limit you set, it serves up the cache page. If not, it generates the page from scratch.

Sounds like some pretty complex coding is required here. Except if you're using CI. If you are, you need to do two things:

Find the `/system/cache` file in your site. It should be empty, except for an `index.html` file. Make sure the folder is writeable—i.e. permissions set to 666, if you're on a Linux system.

Insert, somewhere in a controller function that generates an HTML page, the line:

```
$this->output->cache(5);
```

where 5 is the number of minutes you want your cache to persist before the page is regenerated.

That's it. If you now load the function, you'll see the page load as usual. If you now look at your `/system/cache` folder, however, you'll see a new file in there, with a meaningless title.

Open this up (in a text editor) and you'll see it contains the HTML code for your page, plus a timestamp. If you request the same page again before the timestamp is five minutes old, you'll get the cached page. If you wait longer and the cache file is out of date, your next request will automatically delete it and replace it with a newer version.

If you change your mind about caching the page, delete the `this->output ->cache(5)` line from you controller, and your page will be served up afresh each time. (The last cached file will stay in your `/system/cache` folder until you delete it manually.) If you want to continue caching, but accidentally delete a cache file at any time, don't worry; the system will create a new one when that page is next called.

CI makes this is so quick and simple that it is tempting to cache every page! Just remember that you don't always want to do this: it's best for high load pages that don't change very often, but may not help much on others.

Summary

CI offers you lots of goodies to make coding easier and your websites more professional. This chapter looked at just five of them:

- The text and inflector helpers provide useful functions to manipulate and convert strings.

- The date helper allows you to convert between different date formats and also to cope with time zones.

- The language class makes it easier to write multi-lingual websites, which respond to user preferences. Alas, you still have to do the translation!

- The table class lets you output properly formed HTML tables, directly from a database query if you need to.

- Automatically caching high-load dynamic pages provides a faster response.

11
Using CI to Handle Files and Images

This chapter looks at several useful CI functions and helpers. Each of them is a good example of how a few lines of CI code give you seamless access to a range of applications and actions that would take lots of specialized knowledge to code from scratch. In many cases, CI is simply providing an interface to code classes that were already out there, and which you could download from PEAR or some other source. But CI gives you a standard interface: you just treat it as native CI code, and the framework does all the interfacing stuff for you.

Let's look at five activities in this chapter:

- The file helper makes it easier to write to, and read from files.
- The download helper makes it easy for your website to download files direct to the user, rather than displaying them as HTML.
- The file upload class works the other way, allowing users to put files on your site, with built-in security precautions to limit what they can do.
- The image manipulation class allows you to do several useful things with images, and we'll look at how to resize them and watermark them.
- Lastly, the Zip class allows you to compress files before your users download them.

Each of these examples hides a lot of clever coding and allows you to write practical applications with a minimum of fuss. In many cases, they add extra code to make the activity more robust.

Let's look at them one by one:

The File Helper

PHP's syntax for reading and writing files is not easy to grasp at first sight. CI's file helper contains a few useful functions, which act as a wrapper for PHP's own file handling operations. Start off as always by loading the helper:

```
$this->load->helper('file');
```

Then life gets a lot simpler. For instance, to write to a file, all you need to know is:

- The location of your file.
- The text you want to write to it.
- The mode in which you want to open the file. Modes are defined in the PHP manual (see the page on 'fopen'). They include 'r' for read, 'w' for write (write to the file, overwriting data already there), and 'a' for append (write to the file, adding on to existing data). In each case, adding a '+', say 'a+', opens the file for both read and write operations. 'a' and 'w', but not 'r' or 'r+', also create the file, if one is not already there.

Then you use these three pieces of information as parameters to the `write_file()` function:

```
write_file('e:/filetest.txt', 'hello world', 'a+')
```

This is simpler and more intuitive than PHP's two-step code:

```
if ( $fp = fopen('e:/filetest.txt','r+'))
{
        fwrite($fp, 'hello world');
}
```

Once again, the CI code adds a little extra: it automatically locks the file before writing and unlocks it afterwards. The helper returns 'FALSE' if the file operation doesn't take place, so you can use it to report success or failure. You have to specify a title for your file, but if you don't specify a filepath, it is placed in the web root folder for your site, where your main `index.php` file is.

 Of course, any folder in which you create or write to a file, must have write permissions set. Remember also that if you are running on a Windows system you have to use forward slashes — / — to describe your filepath.

In our application, we can combine this helper with the database utility class. This allows us to create, back up, repair, and optimize databases and tables, though only on MySQL and MySQLi databases. Mix it in with the file helper, and you create a neat backup routine.

```
$this->load->dbutil();
$backup =& $this->dbutil->backup();
$this->load->helper('file');
write_file('e:/mybackup.gz', $backup);
```

The above code writes the latest version of our database to a file on the server.

Reading a file back again is equally simple:

```
$content = read_file('e:/filetest.txt');
```

There's also a function that returns an array of all files and/or folders in a given directory:

```
$filenames = get_filenames('e:/')
```

although, if you use it in a directory with many files, you may find that PHP times out before it can list them all. You can use this in a simple piece of code to check that the files or folders actually in a folder are what you expect. Start by using the CI function to find the files actually present, and a reference array of files you expect to find, then use array_diff() to compare them. Given two arrays, array_diff() tells you what values are in the first that are not in the other, so you have to use it twice, putting each array first.

```
//list files actually found
$files_there = get_filenames('e:/rootfolder/system/application/
                                              controllers');

// list files we expected
$files_expected = array('start.php', 'index.php');

// any found that we didn't expect?
$difference = array_diff($files_there, $files_expected);
echo "<br />Missing files are:";
print_r($difference);

// any expected that we didn't find?
$difference = array_diff($files_expected, $files_there);
echo "<br />Extra files are:";
print_r($difference);
```

Lastly, but far too horrible even to think about, there is the delete_files() function. This deletes all the files within any directory you specify, so that:

```
delete_files('c:/mydirectory/');
```

would delete everything in mydirectory. If you add the optional parameter TRUE, as in:

```
delete_files('c:/mydirectory/', TRUE)?
```

it will also delete all subfolders in that directory Use with great care: just imagine what:

```
delete_files("c:/", TRUE)
```

might do!

The Download Helper

The download helper only has one function, but it complements the file helper very nicely. You might create a file on a website and then want to serve it up to the reader as a file—a text file, for example—rather than converting it into a web page.

A good example would be a database backup file, like the one we created just now for our application.

To recreate the database if it crashes, we need a text file in MySQL's own format. It isn't much use to us to see this on the screen:

```
# # TABLE STRUCTURE FOR: ci_sessions # DROP TABLE IF EXISTS
ci_sessions; CREATE TABLE `ci_sessions` ( `session_id` varchar(40) NOT
NULL default '0', `peopleid` int(11) NOT NULL, `ip_address` varchar(16)
NOT NULL default '0', `user_agent` varchar(50) NOT NULL, `last_activity`
int(10) unsigned NOT NULL default '0', `left` int(11) NOT NULL, `name`
varchar(25) NOT NULL, `status` tinyint(4) NOT NULL default '0' )
ENGINE=MyISAM DEFAULT CHARSET=latin1; INSERT INTO
ci_sessions (session_id, peopleid, ip_address, user_agent, last_activity, left,
name, status) VALUES ('0cc2555fd8f6c6714cab86365f5c6712', 2, '127.0.0.1',
'Mozilla/5.0 (Windows; U; Windows NT 5.0; en-GB; rv', 1168785860, 0,
'David Upton', 9); # # TABLE STRUCTURE FOR: domains # DROP TABLE
IF EXISTS domains; CREATE TABLE `domains` ( `id` int(10) NOT NULL
auto_increment, `url` varchar(100) NOT NULL, `name` varchar(100) NOT
NULL, `registrar` varchar(100) NOT NULL, `dateregd` int(11) NOT NULL
default '0', `cost` float NOT NULL default '0', `regdfor` int(11) NOT NULL
default '0', `notes` blob NOT NULL, `pw` varchar(25) NOT NULL, `un`
```

We need to find a way of downloading it as a file. In other words, if we're working on a Windows system, we want to see this dialogue:

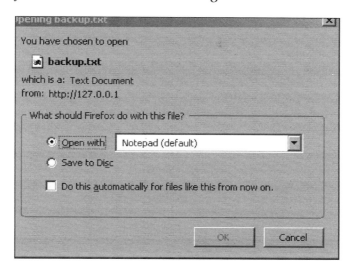

In order to code this over an internet connection, you must specify the type of page you want in the HTTP headers. CI's download helper does this for you in the background. Load the helper with:

```
$this->load->helper('download');
```

and its single method is used like this:

```
force_download($name, $data);
```

where $name is the name you give to the downloaded file and $data is the file contents. If you want to download an existing file, you have to read it into a string first:

```
$data = file_get_contents("e:/mybackup.txt");
$name = 'backup.txt';
force_download($name, $data);
```

The file $data can now be used directly to recreate the MySQL database. You can also use this helper to download reports directly, rather than forcing users to scrape them off the screen.

Behind the scenes, the helper takes care of identifying the MIME type and setting HTTP headers. It relies on one of the 'config' files, `system/application/config/mimes`, which is also used by the Upload class that we'll look at next. This config file stores an array of MIME types and the appropriate HTTP extensions—e.g.:

```
'rtf'  =>      'text/rtf',
'text' =>      'text/plain',
```

which saves you having to remember them!

If you regularly use file types that aren't included on CI's list, you can easily add them to the 'config' file.

The File Upload Class

Sometimes, you want to allow users of your site to upload files. These may be text, or images, or more exotic file types like MP3 audio or MPEG video. This is a more complex process than the file downloads we just discussed, but CI's file upload class takes care of most of the work for you. It also looks after some of the security issues. However, you should always think twice before allowing anyone to upload files to your site, and you may want to protect the upload page to prevent unauthorized users from doing it.

First, you need to allocate space to store the uploaded files—a folder or directory on your server. This must be set with the correct permissions, allowing users to write to it. (i.e. 777 on a Unix/ Linux system). Let's assume you call this folder `uploads`, and put it in your web root folder.

CI's file upload class is loaded with:

```
$this->load->library('upload');
```

Then you need to do three things:

- Set defaults
- Write a controller to handle the uploads
- Provide your user with an upload form and a 'success' form

Let's take them in this order. First, set a series of defaults. You do this by creating a `$config` array.

Let's say you want to set the path to the upload directory you just created. For this, you need to say:

```
$config['upload_path'] = 'uploads';
```

This line can either be in the controller you're about to write, or you can create a config/upload folder to contain it (this would be system/application/config/upload.php).

```
<?php  if (!defined('BASEPATH')) exit('No direct script access
allowed');
$config['upload_path'] = 'uploads';
?>
```

It's important to grasp the difference between these two ways of setting your defaults. If you set the defaults from the config/upload file, you don't need to specifically initialize the file upload class. Just load it and it will find the defaults for itself.

However, if you leave the defaults in the controller, you need to specify where they are when you load the class, using a second parameter to the loading function, like this:

```
$this->load->library('upload', $config);
```

where $config is the name of your array of defaults. (Don't try to set some defaults from the config/upload file and some from the controller!)

OK, so what's this fuss about defaults? So CI sets sensible defaults and you don't need to worry about them, right? Yes, but in this case you do. There are several important ones:

- The location of your upload file: CI doesn't make an assumption about this, you have to tell it.

- The types of file you want to allow your users to upload. This is set like this:
  ```
  $config['allowed_types'] = 'gif|jpg|png';
  ```

  where the acceptable file types are specified with the pipe operator (|) between them. This setting would allow your site to upload the most popular image file types but would not allow it to upload audio files, for example. Setting this is a basic security measure: if you only want images to be uploaded, don't allow people to upload executable files or large MP3s.

  Note that you must set a value before a file type can be uploaded: the default setting (i.e., no setting) allows no files to be uploaded.

- Max_size: it's sensible to set a limit on the maximum size of file, in kilobytes, that can be uploaded. You don't want malicious users filling up all your space. The default setting is 0, which sets no limit.

- Overwrite: if you already have a file in your uploads folder with the same name as the one that a user is uploading, should the old one be overwritten and lost forever? This depends on what your site is doing and why you are allowing uploads. CI defaults to 'FALSE', which means it doesn't overwrite the old file and the new file is saved under a new name. Explicitly set this default to 'TRUE', if you want new files to overwrite the old.

  Note that CI doesn't automatically tell the user that it has renamed his or her file, which may possibly be confusing: see below for how to get at reports on the process.

- You can also set defaults for the size, width, and height of images, for encrypting the file, and for trimming blank spaces from its title.

Now that you have decided on your defaults, you need an upload controller. This is simple. Its role is to initialize the upload class, receive an upload from a user form, and then decide if it has been successful. If yes, it displays a report; if no, it returns to the upload form with a user message. At its simplest, it need only include one active function, do_upload(), like this:

```php
<?php
/*constructor function to initialize controller and load the file
upload class, plus the two other helpers it needs */

class Upload extends Controller {

    function Upload()
    {
        parent::Controller();
        $this->load->helper(array('form', 'url'));
        $this->load->library('upload');
    }

/*now the function which does all the work!*/

function do_upload()
    {
        if ( ! $this->upload->do_upload())
        {
            $error = array('error' =>
                                $this->upload->display_errors());

            $this->load->view('upload_form', $error);
        }
        else
```

```
        {
                $data = array('upload_data' =>
                                        $this->upload->data());
                $this->load->view('upload_success', $data);
        }
    }
}
```

This function needs an `upload_form` view, and an `upload_success` view. To build the first, use the form helper to build a normal form, pointing to the `do_upload` function of our 'upload' controller: but instead of opening it with:

```
echo form_open('upload/do_upload')
```

(as we did in the forms we built in Chapter 5), you open it with the form helper's multipart function:

```
echo form_open_multipart('upload/do_upload');
```

(Remember that we are writing code to produce HTML markup, so we need to echo it to the screen.)

Then, instead of the form helper's `form_input` function, use the `form_upload` function:

```
echo form_upload($data);
```

These two lines of code take care of a lot of really tedious stuff for you.

Add as normal a submit button, and close the form.

```
echo form_submit('mysubmit', 'Submit Post!');
```

Pass your `$view` variable to a view and load it. Your view should also echo the `$error` variable, which the `do_upload` function passed when it loaded the view.

```
echo $error;
```

You should now see something like this:

Clicking on **Browse** allows the user to view the files on her or his own (local) computer, not your server. Once (s)he has selected a file, clicking on upload will call the upload controller, and the file will be transferred to the `upload` folder on your server.

Let's say I try to upload a text file. (Remember that our allowed file types are limited to 'gif | jpg | png'.) I now see:

The filetype you are attempting to upload is not allowed
[_____] Browse...
upload

CI is reporting back the type of error to me: this is the `$this->upload->display_errors()` function in the controller at work, adding an extra variable to the view.

You can also have CI report data on successful uploads to you. As you see, the controller we wrote just now calls a view called `upload_success`, if the upload is successful. The data passed to this view is the contents of the function `$this->upload->data`. This gives you a full array of information about the upload process: possibly more than you would want to display.

Let's say I uploaded a file called `waltzer.jpg`: the default report looks like this:

Your file was successfully uploaded!

- file_name: waltzer1.jpg
- file_type: image/jpeg
- file_path: E:/xampplite/htdocs/packt2/uploads/
- full_path: E:/xampplite/htdocs/packt2/uploads/waltzer1.jpg
- raw_name: waltzer1
- orig_name: waltzer.jpg
- file_ext: .jpg
- file_size: 562.08
- is_image: 1
- image_width: 1600
- image_height: 1200
- image_type: jpeg
- image_size_str: width="1600" height="1200"

Upload Another File!

If you are using your site to create a rival to Flickr, for example, then this amount of information might confuse users who have uploaded their photographs! However, you can easily filter out any information that you don't want in the upload controller.

Please note, by the way, that I set the 'overwrite' default to 'FALSE' when configuring the file upload class to write this example. I then used the code to upload the image file `waltzer.jpg` — twice.

The previous screenshot is CI's report on the second successful upload. You'll see that the file has been renamed `waltzer1.jpg`. If I look in my upload directory, I can see both the original `waltzer.jpg` and the new `waltzer1.jpg` file. Depending on your application, you might want to compare the values for `raw_name` and `orig_name` and inform the user that the file name has been changed.

CI does not compare the two files, only their names. If you are allowing several users to upload files, it is quite possible that two of them will inadvertently use the same filename for different files, and you may not want to lose the first. On the other hand, if you are using the site to upload reports that always have the same name, you may prefer only to have the latest version stored on the site — in which case overwriting is a simple way of saving space.

Here's that image, by the way. We're going to do a lot more with it in the next section.

CI's Image Class

If you are allowing users to upload images to your site, you also need to look at CI's Image Manipulation class. This works with the three most popular image libraries for PHP: GD/GD2, NetPBM, and ImageMagick. (Use `phpinfo()` to find out which of these your server supports.) Image watermarking only works with GD/GD2, though:

The image manipulation class allows you to perform four basic functions with images:

- Resize: You may want to fit them into a standard size on your screen; or you may want to cut them right down to 'thumbnail' images.
- Crop
- Rotate
- Watermark (only available with GD/GD2): This is often used to put a copyright notice on an image, so that people can't simply download it from your site and pass it off as their own work.

Probably the most useful of these functions is resizing, so we'll look at that in a little detail. Cropping and rotating are less useful because you can't do them meaningfully unless you can see the image on the screen. To do this, you need some sort of user interface that allows the user to specify what she or he wants to do and control the way CI implements these functions, and you'll have to build this for yourself!

Let's say you've uploaded your `waltzer.jpg` image, using the file upload class we just discussed, to your `/uploads` folder. (Permissions for this folder have to be set to 777 for you to upload—and also for you to manipulate the images, because CI needs to write the manipulated result back to the folder.)

First, load the library:

```
$this->load->library('image_lib');
```

Then, you need to set a few configuration details. (As with the file upload class, you can either do this in your code, or in a separate `system/application/config/image_lib.php` file.)

There are several preferences you can set and they are listed in the online User Guide. Perhaps the most important are:

- Which image library you are using. The default is GD2, so if you're not using that in your PHP installation, you would need to specify the one you are running, e.g., `$config['image_library'] = 'ImageMagick'` (You'd also have to supply a path to the ImageMagick library using: `$config['library_path'] = '/mypath';`.)
- The image you want to manipulate. This should be the path (relative to your site's root folder) and filename.
- The size you want the image to be after processing—where 'x' is a number of pixels, the width is set by `$config['width'] = x;`, and the height by `$config['height'] = x;`.

These are enough to resize your image, overwriting the old image file with the resized image. The code looks like this:

```
function do_image($image_name)
{
    $this->load->library('image_lib');
    $config['image_library'] = 'GD';
    $config['source_image'] = "$image_name";
    $config['width'] = 75;
    $config['height'] = 50;
    $this->image_lib->initialize($config);
    if(!$this->image_lib->resize())
    {echo "failed";}
    else{echo 'success!';}
}
```

The library can do some other clever things as well. If you don't want to overwrite the original image, specify a new name and filepath for the new version, by adding:

```
$config['new_image'] = 'newfolder/newname.png';
```

Or, if you want to create a thumbnail of the image, simply add:

```
$config['create_thumb'] = TRUE;
```

instead. This has the effect of re-naming the new resized file with a default suffix of _thumb, so that `waltzer.jpg` becomes `waltzer_thumb.jpg`. (You can alter the default suffix as well—see the User Guide.) So you then have two files in the same folder: the original and the thumbnail.

Note that the thumbnail setting doesn't do anything else—you still have to set the size you want it to be.

Here's the image, shrunk right down to 75 by 50 pixels:

An additional function of the image class allows you to watermark images. So, if you've put your own brilliant photograph on your website, you can also add a copyright notice to it.

Once again there are a lot of options, fully explained in the User Guide, but the basic code is simple. Initialize the class, tell it which image you want to watermark and what you want the watermark to say, and call the watermark function.

```
function wm_image()
{
    $this->load->library('image_lib');
    $config['source_image'] = 'uploads/waltzer.jpg';
    $config['wm_text'] = 'Copyright 2007 - David Upton';
    $config['wm_type'] = 'text';
    $this->image_lib->initialize($config);
    if (!$this->image_lib->watermark())
            {echo 'failure to watermark';}
    else {echo 'success';}

}
```

(The wm_type option set to text allows you to watermark with text. Otherwise, set this option to overlay, and supply an image, which will be superimposed on your original image.)

This is what the image looks like now.

My actual code was slightly more complex than the example shown above, so that I could control the size and positioning of my watermark to make it more easily visible on this page. The default code shown above would be adequate for most purposes, but the watermark comes out too small to be clear on a printed page. See CI's online User Guide for more information about working with external fonts.

This class is beautifully simple to use, and it's only when you look at the underlying code in the image manipulation library (in the file system/libraries/Image_lib. php) that you realize how much complex coding CI has spared you!

Easy File Compression with the CI Zip Class

If you're moving around large files like images, you might need to compress them. CI contains a handy library for doing this.

Let's take the photograph we've already used: `waltzer.jpg`. It's on our `/uploads` folder.

As always, you start by initializing the Zip class. Once you've done that, you have to tell CI which file you want to zip, and create an archive to put it in. Then you use the `read_file` function to read it in and zip it, and the download function to download it to your desktop.

```
function zip_image()
{
    $this->load->library('zip');
    $this->zip->archive('my_backup.zip');
    $path = 'uploads/waltzer1.jpg';
    $this->zip->read_file($path);
    $this->zip->download('my_backup.zip');
}
```

The CI Zip encoding class is more complex than this and allows you several options. As usual, they're all set out in the online User Guide. But this should give you an idea of how easy CI makes it to zip downloads from your site, minimizing the bandwidth they consume and saving time for your users.

Summary

This chapter collects together a few CI helpers and classes with similar themes. They help you to:

- Write and read files on your system, with minimal coding, while CI locks and unlocks the files in the background.

- Download files rather than show them as HTML on the screen, with CI providing the HTTP headers and worrying about MIME types for you.

- Upload files to your site, allowing you to specify security constraints like the size and type of files you allow.

- Easily manipulate images, to resize or watermark them.

- Compress your files before you download them to your users.

This to me is what frameworks are all about. Instead of a lot of tedious coding, they let you get on with building an application that works. They give you a standard and easy interface, and they worry about the details for you.

12

Production Versions, Updates, and Big Decisions

The great day has come. Your development site is running well enough on your local development for you to transfer it to a production site hosted on a remote web server. It should be easy to do this. Copy over all the files, including the whole of the system folder, update the config settings, copy over and link to the database, and away you go. Sometimes, it really is that easy.

But when it isn't, it's always the night before you are giving an all-important presentation to a venture capitalist or a major prospect. So, in case this happens to you, this chapter covers:

- What to look for in your config files
- Some diagnostic tools to use if you get stuck
- Some potential differences between servers that may trip you up
- Some notes on security, now that you're out there in the big world

Next, this chapter covers upgrading, and looks at some of the ways in which CI has changed in the year it's been available. How stable is it? What decisions should you make if you are committing a critical site to it? And what should you do, once your site is up and running, if Rick Ellis brings out a newer version of CI?

Lastly, we briefly discuss making your own alterations to the core of CI. It's all there; it's open-source it's possible. Whether it's sensible or not is another matter.

Connections: Check the Config Files

Systems usually fail at the interfaces. That's what your config files are there for: to give you a place to put all those interfaces. If you haven't done so, you've missed one of CI's major strengths.

The major interface problems are likely to be:

URLs

CI works by finding files. Your user connects to `index.php`, and then a whole process of loading starts. At least, it should do. Make sure you have set the web address and server addresses correctly in your config files. The web address is your web root folder; you may have to ask your ISP for the server address, though usually it is clear from their own 'file manager' programme.

I've had particular issues trying to run sub-domains. Many hosts allow them, but map the domains to folders in ways you don't expect.

Databases

Locating and connecting to your database is often a major issue. Look at your `config` file and your `config/database` file. You need to make sure that you have the correct site and server addresses, and the correct database name, address, user name, and password. Be careful with prefixes—sometimes these are added automatically. (Your site is called 'fred'. Your database, you think, is called 'mydata' and your user name is 'mylogin'. But the server thinks they are called 'fred_mydata', 'fred_mylogin', etc.)

Sometimes, it helps to create a new user on your database, even if you have one already, and set the log-in for this user's name and password. I have no idea why this works, but it does.

In the config file, you can set CI to accept different types of URI protocols, which determine how the server handles the URI string. The default is:

```
$config['uri_protocol'] = "auto";
```

but there are four other options that you can try if this doesn't work. If the correct option isn't set, you may find your site partly works, but (for example) forms don't call the target page.

Other config Files

The `config/routes` file sets the default path the application follows, if the user doesn't specify a controller/method through the URL (i.e. if they just log on to `www.mysite.com`). This should normally be set at the default:

```
$route['default_controller'] = 'index';
```

If you renamed the `system` folder, then remember that you also need to alter the `index.php` file in the site's root directory. The default setting is:

```
$system_folder = "system";
```

Look Out for PHP 4/5 and Operating System Differences

CI should be able to live with any version of PHP including and later than 4.3. However, this doesn't mean that any PHP code you write will also be compatible—so if you wrote it on Xampplite using PHP 5, and are moving to an ISP with a PHP 4 server, look out for problems due to language differences.

PHP (of whatever version) can be set up in different ways. It's worth running `phpinfo()` on your local and remote sites, and checking for differences.

Case sensitivity is different between Microsoft and Linux servers. So if you've developed your site on a PC, and then uploaded it to a Linux-based server, expect the server to report that it can't find some of the models or libraries you want to load. If you've checked and they have been uploaded, then make sure that the capitalization is correct. Because class definitions and constructors in CI have to begin with a capital, it's easy to begin the file name with a capital too. If you load a model, say, inside a controller, and give it a capitalized name (`$this->load->Mymodel`), then Windows and Linux may have different views about calls to `$this->mymodel`.

As an extreme example of server differences, I once began to write a controller, decided to make it a model instead, and so saved it in the `model` folder without realizing that I had left the first few lines as:

```
class Myclass extends Controller {

    function Myclass()
    {
            parent::Controller();
```

instead of changing them to:

```
class Myclass extends Model {

    function Myclass()
    {
        parent::Model();
```

Running locally on Xampplite, this did not throw an exception. Transferred to a remote Linux server, it immediately failed (and you can imagine how long it took to track down…).

Some PHP functions also appear to behave differently on different operating systems: for instance, include_once() is case insensitive on Windows but not on other systems. That's not specifically a CI issue, though.

Also, your database may be a different version—many ISPs are very traditional, running MySQL 3.23 for instance! This seems to cause some incompatibilities, which means that uploading a database by a SQL query is less easy than it should be. (For instance, it may not accept comments on db tables.)

Linux has a different system of file permissions to Windows. Make sure that you have the correct permissions on your files and folders. Certain CI file permissions must be set correctly before the system can work.

Diagnostic Tools

The first line of the index.php file is:

```
error_reporting(E_ALL);
```

which displays any PHP errors on your screen, like this:

A PHP Error was encountered

Severity: Warning

Message: Cannot modify header information - headers already sent by (output started at E:\xampplite\htdocs\packt2\system\application\libraries\errors.php:35)

Filename: libraries/Session.php

Line Number: 282

Obviously, error reports like this look bad, and may give hackers too much information, so for the production version you alter this to:

```
error_reporting(0);
```

But then, any problems may simply result in a blank screen, with no helpful diagnostic information. You may have to turn error reporting back on, until you have got the site running. One compromise is to set it to an intermediate level, such as:

```
error_reporting(E_ERROR);
```

This will prevent 'warnings' but will still give you information about serious problems. 'Warnings' are usually conditions that don't stop the programme from executing, but may point to other underlying issues that you hadn't considered.

The CI Profiler class—see Chapter 8—is also very useful: it shows you what queries you are doing, and what is in the POST array.

Various other tools I have found useful when things don't work:

1. Set CI to print a log file. (Done from the config file—see Chapter 8—you need to set:

   ```
   $config['log_threshold'] = 4;
   ```

   4 shows all messages, including just notices and warnings; sometimes these are pointers to an underlying problem. Then look at the log (printed in /system/logs, filed by date.) This will tell you which parts of the CI system have been called, so you can at least see where the process stopped. (Set the value back to 0 to prevent further logging. Remember to do this, and to remove the log files when you've finished: it's amazing how much space they take up.)

2. If you can access them, print out the PHP server and session variables:

   ```
   print_r($_SERVER)
   ```

   and:

   ```
   print_r($_SESSION)
   ```

and use them to check that the document_root and script_filename values are what you expect. If not, you may need to adjust your config file values for base_url and server You can also see if there is an [HTTP_COOKIE] value set, which will show you if your session class is enabled and working.

3. Check what CI has loaded into its superobject by using PHP's methods:

   ```
   get_declared_classes();
   ```

   and:

   ```
   get_class_methods();
   ```

4. CI's own `show_error()` function is only a means of formatting error reports that you generate. So including the following line in your code, say at some branch that should not be reached:

```
show_error('test of error function');
```

would result in your screen showing:

> An Error Was Encountered
>
> test of error function

I don't find that very useful. What I want is a system that will give me full, helpful error reports, when and where I want them, but won't show them when I don't want them to appear. I wrote my own function, which reads:

```
function reportme($file, $line, $message)
{
   $obj =& get_instance();
   if(isset($_POST))
          {$bert = print_r($_POST, TRUE);}
   else {$bert = 'no post array';}
   if(isset($_SESSION))
          {$sid = print_r($_SESSION, TRUE);}
   else{$sid = 'no session array';}

    $time = Gmdate("H:i j-M-Y");
/*full report*/
    $errorstring =  "$time - $file - $line: $message: POST array:
$bert SESSION array: $sid\n";

/*short report*/
   $shortstring =  "$file - $line: $message";

/*set $setting to 'test' if you want to write to the screen*/
   $setting = 'test';
   if($setting == 'test')
          {echo $errorstring;}

/*set $action to 'log' if you want to log errors*/
   $action = 'log';
   if($action == 'log')
          {
          $filename = $obj->config->item('errorfile');
          $fp = fopen("$filename", "a+")or die("cant open file");
          fwrite($fp, $errorstring);
```

```
    fclose($fp);
    }
}
```

This lives in a library called `errors`. I have to remember to load the library, and then, whenever I have a section of code that I'm not confident about, I include the function:

```
$this->errors->reportme(__FILE__,__LINE__,'if the code has reached
here it is because......');
```

I can then set the `reportme()` function to give me a report on the screen, or in my log file.

There are several advantages to a simple method like this. Firstly, I can alter the `reportme()` function easily, to make it write errors to a file, or to do nothing at all: so I can make all my reports disappear from the screen at once, or come back again, by changing one line of code.

Secondly, let's say I am expecting a variable to have a particular value. (An ID number to be an integer, say.) I make the message as complete and helpful as possible. I try to say what I expected to find (an integer), as well as including the value I actually got. The function call also uses PHP's __FILE__ and __LINE__ 'magic constants' to tell me exactly where it happened.

So, if this particular piece of code becomes a problem when I transfer it to another server, possibly some time after I wrote it, I can immediately find the code, and the text helps me to remember why it is a problem. Six months after you write code, you can't just pick it up straight away, especially if it is late at night and a client is on the phone asking for an explanation! The more helpful the error text, the easier it is to respond sensibly.

Thirdly, if the integrity of the site was really critical, I could set the function to email me with error reports. That might result in a very full mailbox during the development phase, but once the site is stable and in use, it might be very useful to have an immediate warning if the site is experiencing problems. You will know about them before your users tell you.

Coping with Change in New CI Versions

Between 28 February 2006 and 30 October 2006, CI went from its first beta to version 1.5. That's a pretty impressive rate of development.

During that time Rick Ellis made several fairly radical changes, particularly to the structure of the site. For the most part, he has been careful to make them backwardly compatible—but not all of them are. If you are new to CI and have downloaded the latest version, you can skip this section. But if you wrote programmes using earlier versions, you may need to check these changes. You may also need to check if you are using CI libraries or plug-ins written by other people.

Rick has grappled with two main problems:

How to Load Models, and What to Call Them

At first, there were no models, just folders for `scripts` and `libraries`. There was no provision to initialize them automatically as part of the CI 'super-object'. As a result, you had an MVC system without 'model' files, which seems confusing.

As well as this, there are two `libraries` folders: `/system/application/libraries` holds any files you write for yourself, while `/system/libraries` holds the system's own operating files. This may have confused a few people: the two are quite different! You ought to be adding to or altering the former; you probably don't need to alter the latter. (And if you do, you run serious risks of incompatibility if you upgrade to a later CI version: see below.)

With version 1.3 came a new 'model' class. The User Guide defines models as, "PHP classes that are designed to work with information in your database". When first introduced, CI models connected automatically to the database. However, since Version 1.3.3, you must specifically load the database from inside the model or the controller that calls it.

Or, when you call the model from the controller, you can do so in this format:

```
$this->load->model('Mymodel', '', TRUE);
```

and then the 'TRUE' loads the model with the default database connection made, as defined in your config file. (The second parameter, left blank here, is an optional alias for the model.)

CI will probably still work if you put the functionality of a 'model' (in the MVC sense) into a 'library' or a (deprecated) 'script', as you had to in the early days when there were no 'models' folders: but you'll have to access the CI resources differently—see the next section!

How to Initialize Your Own 'library' Classes

Originally, you couldn't make your own classes part of the CI 'super-object'. This was a problem, because it meant that your library code couldn't, for instance, access the database through Active Record, or use other CI libraries, and that became pretty limiting.

Version 1.2 added the `get_instance()` function that allows you to access the 'super-object'. (See Chapter 7.) You could include it in your 'library' or 'script' and then use the CI resources. (Unless your new file was a functional script rather than an OO class, of course. However, script files are probably best used for simple low-level functions.)

Version 1.4 introduced a new system. You had to create two files for each 'library' class. The first was the class itself, say `Newclass.php`, stored in the `application/libraries` folder, and the second, stored in an `application/init` folder, had to be called `init_newclass.php` and contained a few standard lines of code that initialized it as part of the 'super-object'. However, you still had to use the `get_instance()` function to access CI resources.

In version 1.5, the `init` folder has been deprecated, and initialization happens automatically. You now only need the one file for each 'library' class.

The old `scripts` folder has also been deprecated. 'Deprecate' in this context, usually means that the thing concerned is till recognized and should still work, but that the developer offers no guarantee that it will do so in all future versions. In other words, don't panic if you still have scripts in a `system/application/scripts` folder—but don't write any more.

If you are planning to use libraries or plug-ins written by the CI community, please check first that they are up to date with the latest CI version. There are quite a few around still that were written for 1.4.1 and have separate 'init' files. Updating them isn't difficult, but it does take some care to get it right.

So Should I Update If a New CI Version Comes Out?

New versions of CI come out from time to time. They come with comprehensive instructions for updating. Usually, this involves copying a new set of files to your `system` folder. Sometimes, you need to change config files, or your `index.php` file, as well, but none of these are major changes and none of them are rocket science. Because the folder structure keeps your application files in their own place, it's usually easy to update the system without touching the applications.

But, say you've written your killer app in version 1.5. It's uploaded to your production system and working fine. Then, Rick Ellis brings out CI version 1.6 (or 2.8 or whatever...). It has interesting new features, and some bug fixes. Do you upgrade to it?

I would say, 'Yes', if it's a minor upgrade, say between 1.5.2 and 1.5.3. But if it's a major version change, and your existing system is working, leave well alone. You can tell the difference partly from the numbering, but also from the 'change log' published with each upgrade when it comes out. The sort of changes that have been made in CI over the last year fall into three categories:

Bug fixes: There are surprisingly few of these—CI is excellent code, and most of the base classes have been well tested by hundreds if not thousands of users.

New features:. These appear regularly, but if you managed to build your application without them, will they really be helpful now?

Subtle changes: As I've described, CI has gone through a process of internal evolution, and it may well continue to do so. As you can see from the following table, some of these might be backwardly compatible, or they might require fairly major re-writes of your code.

Some changes between versions of CI:

Version	Change Log
1.2	Added a global function named `get_instance()` allowing the main CodeIgniter object to be accessible throughout your own classes.
1.3	Added support for Models.
1.3	Added the ability to pass your own initialization parameters to your custom core libraries when using `$this->load->library()`.
1.3	Added better class and function name-spacing to avoid collisions with user developed classes. All CodeIgniter classes are now prefixed with *CI_* and all controller methods are prefixed with *_ci* to avoid controller collisions.
1.3.3	Models do not connect automatically to the database as of this version.
1.4	Added the ability to replace core system classes with your own classes.
1.4	Updated the Models loader function to allow multiple loads of the same model.
1.4.1	Updated plugins, helpers, and language classes to allow your `application` folder to contain its own plugins, helpers, and language folders. Previously, they were always treated as global for your entire installation. If your `application` folder contains any of these resources they will be used instead the global ones.

Version	Change Log
1.4.1	Deprecated the `application/scripts` folder. It will continue to work for legacy users, but it is recommended that you create your own libraries or models instead. It was originally added before CI had user libraries or models, but it's not needed anymore.
1.5	Added the ability to extend libraries and extend core classes, in addition to being able to replace them.
1.5	Deprecated `init` folder. Initialization happens automatically now.

Don't misunderstand me. All of these are sensible changes and all of them are improvements. If you are starting a new project, start with the latest CI version. But if you wrote code using version 1.3, say, you will find that your `scripts` folder is deprecated and your models don't automatically connect to the database any more. Personally, I would leave that code running on version 1.3 of CI, rather than try to upgrade it. Life's too short.

How to Add On to CI's Basic Classes

Normal users are unlikely to need to alter the base CI classes. It's a pretty good framework, it does a lot of things, and after all, the point of a framework is to make thing easy, right? However, if you must ....

CI is open source, and you can see all the code as soon as you download it. This includes the basic libraries that make CI work (stored in `system/libraries`) as well as the ones you wrote in `system/application/libraries`.) So it has always been possible to change CI any way you like.

Changing system library files has two problems, however:

- There's no guarantee that your new code will be compatible with the rest of CI, or with updated versions. This may lead to subtle or strange errors that won't be easy to track down.

- If you later update your CI version, the `system` folder is likely to be changed. The library file you altered may well be over-written and updated, so you'd have to go through your changes and transfer them to the updated version.

However, since version 1.5, there are now two sensible 'work-arounds' for tinkering with the CI library classes (except for the underlying 'database' and 'controller' classes, which you touch at your peril.)

- Firstly, you can create a file with the same name as any of the system base classes in your /system/application folder. The system then uses this one, in preference to the standard one in the /system folder. This requires exact naming conventions—see the online User Guide. It also requires you to copy all the functionality in the existing class as well as your own additions or changes.

- Secondly, and more conveniently, you can create a new class that extends the system class. (So it's perhaps best referred to as a 'sub-class'.) Again, there are naming conventions—see the online User Guide. Extending the underlying system class means that your new sub-class inherits all the resources of the underlying CI class, but adds a few extra methods of your own. This should mean that, if you update your CI version, the underlying CI class will be replaced, but your new sub-class (which you should put in the system/application folder) will be left untouched.

However, neither of these methods will guarantee that your code is (or remains) compatible with the rest of CI.

Looking through the CI online forums, there are various suggestions for extending the Validation, Unit Testing, and Session classes. Unit Testing, for example, only has two functions and a limited number of comparisons. Perhaps you want a function to show up errors in red, so they stand out when the test results are returned?

If you wanted to make extensive use of some other testing function, it would be simpler to add it in via a sub-class, extending Unit Testing, than to write it out in the controller each time you called Unit Testing.

If you wanted to do this, you'd start your new sub-class this way:

```
class MY_Unit_test extends CI_Unit-test {
    function My_Unit_test()
    {
        parent::CI_Unit_test();
    }

    function newfunction()
    {
            //new code here!
    }
}
}
```

Notice three things here:

- The name of the underlying unit testing class is `CI_Unit_test`, even though the filename of the class code is `system/libraries.unit_test`.

- If you need to use a constructor in your sub-class, make sure you extend the parent constructor first, as here.

- Your new sub-class name should be prefixed with `MY_`, and saved as `application/libraries/MY_unit_test.php`. (Unlike the main classes, where the `CI_` prefix is part of the class name but not of the filename, here the `MY_` prefix is part of both.)

Once you've created your sub-class, you load it like this:

```
$this->load->library('unit_test');
```

In other words, exactly the same as before you wrote the sub-class; and you call a function in the same way too, except that this time you can call not only the existing unit test functions, but also any new ones you've written yourself:

```
$this->unit_test->newfunction();
```

When you next update your CI installation, the unit test library in the `system` folder will be overwritten, but the one in the `application` folder won't, so your code will still be there. Of course, you'll need to check that the updated system library is still compatible with your own code.

Summary

In this chapter, we've seen some of things that can go wrong when you try to transfer your system from a local server to a remote one. This may involve:

- A different version of PHP or MySQL
- A different operating system

In particular, we've looked at case sensitivity, PHP differences, and MySQL issues. We've also looked at diagnostic tools.

Then we looked at the CI's updates. These have all been major improvements, but my advice is, if you have a system working on the current CI version and a new one comes out, think carefully before you upgrade.

Lastly, we looked at the pros and cons of adding to CI's basic classes. Most users won't need to do this, but if you want to, I strongly suggest that the best way to do it is to sub-class an existing library class.

13
Instant CRUD—or Putting it All Together

The most essential—and the most boring—part of writing any dynamic site is the CRUD. You have one or more database tables; you need to be able to Create, Read, Update, and Delete entries on each of these. Later on, you'll do clever things with the data, but until there is some user-friendly way to put it there and maintain it, your site isn't viable.

But this involves writing CRUD functions and these, though conceptually quite easy, are fairly complex and time-consuming. So for our site, I've written a generalized CRUD model, using CI's classes and helpers to make it easier. In this chapter, you'll see how this model works and how to integrate it into our application.

The CRUD model does more than just CRUD. It validates user-entered data, and also checks it in several ways—e.g., to see that you don't do a 'delete' operation without limiting it to a specific table row, or that you don't accidentally repeat 'create' operations by going back to the entry form and reloading it in your browser.

Lastly, the CRUD model contains its own self-testing framework, so that you can perform development tests as you build or adapt your code.

There are other CRUD frameworks out there, which may be more comprehensive and possibly better code (see Chapter 15). However, this one does work. And it's a good way of summing up and using many of the lessons that we've learned in the previous chapters.

This chapter sets out the code for the model, with some comments:

- First of all, we look at the design philosophy.
- Then we look at a standard controller to use with the model.
- Then we look at the way database tables must be structured.

- Then we'll look at the model itself: firstly, the array that holds information about the database, and then at the separate functions.

- Lastly, we'll look at the self-test functions.

The CRUD Model: Design Philosophy

The idea behind this CRUD model is that it can be called by any controller for any table. The data about that table, and how you want its update form displayed is held once, in an array. Everything else is standard: the controller just identifies itself (and thereby the table it acts on) and if necessary, gives an ID number for a record. So all you have to do is write a few simple controllers, and all the work of setting out forms and making database connections is done for you.

Remember that the user can't talk to a model directly, so (s)he has to go through a controller every time. You could put all the code in the controller, but then you'd have to copy it all for each new controller. This way, there is only one set of CRUD code in the model, so only one set to update and maintain. The price is that you have to keep passing information backwards and forwards between controllers and model, which makes the code slightly more difficult to follow.

For the sake of simplicity, I've used two external functions that aren't defined in this code:

- `failure()`, which reports errors; however, I want this done.

- A model called `display` — this creates menus and sets up base URLs and so on. So all the CRUD functions build up a pile of data, put it in the `$data` variable, and simply call:

```
$this->display->mainpage($data);
```

I also want the CRUD model to be able to test itself, so it includes a self-test suite. Calling this during the design process allows me to check that the model will behave as I want it to, under any conditions I can think of. (It's surprising how writing the test suite makes you realize new things that can go wrong — but better now than when your clients use the site.)

Please bear in mind that every model like this is a compromise. The more you ask of it, the more it asks of you. For instance, this model won't work unless your database tables are laid out in specific ways. It will lay out forms in quite sophisticated ways, but it is not infinitely flexible. It doesn't include JavaScript for better control of the user's experience. It can't handle exceptions to its own rules. On the other hand, provided you only want to do a set of standard things (that are pretty common), it makes life a lot easier.

The Standard Controller Format

Firstly, for each database table, you need a standard controller. This is how the user will interact with your table—e.g., to add a new site, change the details of an existing one, etc. To add a new person, the user will interact with the `people` table, so we need a different controller: but it is almost the same as the `sites` controller.

This is the controller for our `sites` table:

```php
<?php
class Sites extends Controller {

/*the filename, class name, constructor function names and this
variable are the only thing you need to change: to the name of the
table/controller (First letter in upper case for the Class name and
constructor function, lower case for the file and variable.lower
case!)*/
    var $controller    = 'sites';

/*constructor function*/
    function Sites()
    {
        parent::Controller();
        $this->load->model('crud');
    }

/*function to update an entry (if an ID is sent) or to insert a new
one. Also includes validation, courtesy of CI */
    function insert($id)
    {
        $this->crud->insert($this->controller, $id);
    }

/*interim function to pass post data from an update or insert through
to Crud model, which can't receive it directly*/
    function interim()
    {
        $this->crud->insert2($this->controller, $_POST);
    }

/*function to delete an entry, needs table name and id. If called
directly, needs parameters passed to function; if not, from Post
array*/
    function delete($idno=0, $state='no')
    {
        if(isset($_POST['id'])&& $_POST['id'] > 0)
            {$idno = $_POST['id'];}
        if(isset($_POST['submit']))
            {$state = $_POST['submit'];}
```

```
                $this->crud->delete($this->controller, $idno, $state);
      }
  /*function to show all entries for a table*/
    function showall()
    {
                $this->crud->showall($this->controller, $message);
    }


  /*function to show all data in a table, but doesn't allow any
  alterations*/
    function read()
    {
                $this->crud->read($this->controller);
    }

  /*function to set off the test suite on the 'crud' model. This
  function need only appear in one controller, as these tests are made
  on a temporary test table so that your real data is not affected*/
    function test()
    {
    $this->crud->test();
    }
}
?>
```

As you see, this is pretty lean and completely generalized. If you wanted to make it the people controller instead of the sites controller — in other words, to allow you to create, read, update or delete entries in the people table, all you need to do is:

- Change the class name from Sites to People (upper-case initial letter!).
- Change the $controller variable from sites to people (lower case).
- Change the constructor function name from Sites to People (upper case initial letter).
- Save the new controller as:
  system/application/controllers/people.php.

The name of the controller must be exactly the same as the name of the database table to which it relates — so for the people table, it must be people. The name must have an uppercase first letter in the class definition line and the constructor function, but nowhere else.

The Database Tables

There are three simple rules for your database tables:

1. The main ID field in each table must always be called 'id' and must be an auto-incrementing field. (This is a standard MySQL field type. It automatically creates a new, unique number each time you make a new entry.)

2. There must also be a field called 'name' in every table, if you want to use it as the basis for a dynamic drop-down box on any form.

3. You also need a 'submit' field for holding states, and things like that.

Otherwise you can have whatever fields you like, and name them anything your database system is happy with. Everything else is handled by the CRUD model, for any controller/table pair designed along these lines.

The Heart of the Model: the Array

Preliminaries over. Let's start on the CRUD model.

First, you need to define the CRUD model and a constructor function. Standard stuff by now:

```php
<?php
class Crud extends Model {
/*create the array to pass to the views*/
    var $data = array();
    var $form = array();
    var $controller;


    function Crud()
    {
        // Call the Model constructor
        parent::Model();
        $this->load->helper('form');
        $this->load->helper('url');
        $this->load->library('errors');
        $this->load->library('validation');
        $this->load->database();
        $this->load->model('display');
```

Save it as `system/application/models/crud.php`.

Then comes the boring bit, but you only have to do it once. You need to write a multi-dimensional array. (I started to learn PHP from a book—it had better be nameless—which said 'multi-dimensional arrays aren't encountered very often, so we won't go into them in further detail here'. I seem to have been using them ever since.)

The first dimension of our array is the list of tables. (`sites`, `people`, etc.)

The second dimension is the list of fields within each table. For the `sites` tables, these are `id`, `name`, `url`, etc.)

The third dimension describes each field and provides a set of parameters that control how it will be handled by the insert/update form. These are:

- The text you want the user to see on the insert form: how this field is described to a human, rather than its actual name. (So the first one is `ID number of this site` rather than just `id`.) This is to help you to make your forms user-friendly.

- The type of form object you want to use to display this field on your insert/ update form: this might be an input box, or a text area, or a drop-down box. (This CRUD model covers some but not all of the options.)

- Any CI validation rules you want to impose when the user fills out this form. This can be left blank.

- If you want to display this field as a dynamic drop-down box, the name of the table it will draw on. See below for explanation. This can also be left blank.

We've already declared the array as a class variable `$form`, so ever afterwards we have to refer to it as `$this->form`). It is defined inside the constructor, that is, it follows on immediately from the previous code.

```
$this->form =
array
('sites' => array
(
'id'        => array('ID number of this site',
                'readonly', 'numeric'),
'name'      => array('Name of site', 'textarea',
                'alpha_numeric'),
'url'       => array('Qualified URL,
                eg http://www.example.com', 'input', ''),
'un'        => array('username to log in to site',
                'input', 'numeric|xss_clean'),
'pw'        => array('password for site', 'input',
                'xss_clean'),
```

```
'client1'       => array('Main client',
                    'dropdown', '', 'people' ),
'client2'       => array('Second client', 'dropdown',
                    '', 'people'),
'admin1'        => array('First admin', 'dropdown',
                    '', 'people'),
'admin2'        => array( 'Second Admin', 'dropdown',
                    '', 'people'),
'domainid'      => array('Domain name', 'dropdown',
                    'numeric', 'domains'),
'hostid'        => array( 'Host', 'dropdown',
                    'numeric', 'hosts'),
'submit'        => array( 'Enter details', 'submit', 'mumeric')
                ),
'domains' => array
    (
    'id'        => array('ID number of this domain',
                    'hidden', 'numeric'),
//etc etc etc!!
```

You can see that, within the $form array, there are sub-arrays for each table (here, sites and domains, though I only just started the latter, for space reasons) which each contain their own sub-sub-arrays, one for each field ('id', 'name', etc). Each of these sub-sub-arrays is in turn an array that contains the three or four values we described above.

It can be fiddly to get the array syntax right, but conceptually it is simple.

For the complete set of tables in our application, this array takes about 120 lines to specify. But you only have to do it once! This is the heart of your model. End the constructor function with a closing bracket '}', and go on to the other functions in the CRUD model.

If you ever need to change your database tables (add a new field, for instance) or you want to change your validation rules, then you need only change the values in this array. Everything else will change automatically: for instance, next time you try to add a new entry, you should see the entry form reflecting the change.

Function by Function: the CRUD Model

The various functions that make up the CRUD model are as follows:

Showall

This is the function that the user will go to most often. It acts as an entry point for all the other operations — make a new entry, update, or delete an entry. It shows you what is already in the table. With some test data in the `sites` table, it looks like this:

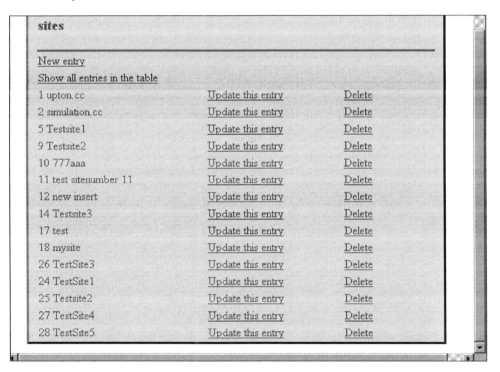

As you can see, from this screen you can update the entry for a site, or delete it. You can also make a new entry, or read all the data in the table.

By the way, please bear in mind that this model doesn't include any security provisions. In a real site, you might want to fine-tune users' options — e.g., allow them to update but not delete. And you would want to make sure that hackers couldn't access the functions of the CRUD model by typing in URLs like www.example.com/index.php/sites/delete/18. CI's URL-based structure makes it relatively easy to deduce how the system accesses these commands, so you might want to ensure that the user has to be logged in to the site before the CRUD model will activate at all.

Right, back to the CRUD mechanisms. Remember that humans can't call the model directly. In each case the option (to delete, update, etc.) is exercised via a call to the controller. Just to jump back, the `sites` controller that called up the `showall` function did so with this line of code:

```
$this->crud->showall($this->controller);
```

in other words, it substituted `sites` for `$this->controller`, and passed that value as a parameter to the CRUD function, to tell it which controller it was acting for.

Let's now look at the `showall` function. It has been passed its first parameter, `sites`. We'll leave `$message` until later. Concentrate on the highlighted lines.

```
    /*this function lists all the entries in a database table on one
page. Note that every db table must have an 'id' field and a 'name'
field to display!
This page is a jumping-off point for the other functions - ie to
create, read, update or delete an entry.
When you've done any of these, you are returned to this page. It has a
'message' parameter, so you can return with a message - either success
or failure.*/

function showall($controller='', $message = '', $test ='no')
{
        $result = '';
        $mysess = $this->session->userdata('session_id');
        $mystat = $this->session->userdata('status');
        if(!$this->db->table_exists($controller))
            {
            $place =    __FILE__ . __LINE__;
            $outcome = "exception:$place:looking for table
$controller: it doesn't exist'";
/*test block: what if there is no controller by that name?*/
                if($test =='yes')
                    {
                      return $outcome;
                    }
                else{
                    $this->failure($outcome, 'sites');
                    }
                }
/*end test block*/
        $this->db->select('id, name');
        $query = $this->db->get($controller);
        if ($query->num_rows() > 0)
            {
            $result .= "<table class='table'>";
```

```
                $result .= "<tr><td colspan='3'><h3>$controller</h3></
                                                td></tr>";
                $result .= "<tr><td colspan='3' class='message'>
                                        $message</td></tr>";
                $result .= "<tr><td colspan='3'>";
                $result .= anchor("$controller/insert/0", 'New entry');
                $result .= "</td></tr>";
                $result         .= "<tr><td colspan='3'>";
                $result .= anchor("$controller/read",
                                'Show all entries in the table');
                $result .= "</td></tr>";
                foreach ($query->result() as $row)
                        {
                        $result .= "<tr><td>";
                        $result .= $row->id;
                        $result .= " ";
                        $result .= $row->name;
                        $result .= "</td><td>";
                        $result .= anchor("$controller/insert/
                                        $row->id",'Update this entry');
                        $result .= "</td><td>";
                        $result .= anchor("$controller/delete/
                                                $row->id",'Delete');
                        $result .= "</td></tr>";
                        }
                $result .= "</table>";

                $data['text'] = $result;
                $this->display->mainpage($data, $this->status);
                }
        else
                {$place = __FILE__ . __LINE__;
                $outcome = "exception: $place:
                                        no results from table $controller";
/*test block: were there results from this table/ controller?*/
                if($test == 'yes')
                        {$place = __FILE__ . __LINE__;
                        return $outcome;
                        }
/*end test block*/
                else{
                        $message = "No data in the $controller table";
/*note: this specific exception must return to another controller
which you know does contain data…… otherwise, it causes an infinite
loop! */
                        $this->failure($message, 'sites');
                        }
                }
        }
```

It sets up a table, displaying some data (`id` and `name`) about each entry. Each entry line also gives you the option to update or delete the entry: this is achieved using CI's `anchor` function to create hyperlinks to the appropriate functions in the appropriate controller.

There's also a single line that offers you the opportunity to create a new site, again by offering a hyperlink to the controller's `insert` function. (Note: I've called the `insert` function both for making new entries and updating old ones. This is because the model assumes that if `insert` is called with an ID number, it is to update the corresponding entry. If it's called without an ID number, it creates a new entry.)

A lot of the code is taken up with exception handling: what if the table doesn't exist, what if the query returns no information? Exceptions are passed to the failure function. There are also two test blocks to allow me to run self-tests.

In addition, there's a line that allows you to read (but not alter) all the data in the tables. Let's look at the read function first, as it's the simplest.

Reading the Data

I've used CI's HTML Table (see Chapter 10) and Active Record classes (see Chapter 4) to show just how simple this piece of functionality is. I want a simple formatted page that shows all the data in the database in an HTML table. It doesn't allow any changes: it is literally the 'read' page.

First there has to be a function in the controller to call the model and tell the model which controller/table is to be displayed. That's the `read()` function in the standard controller.

It calls the following function in the CRUD model:

```
/*queries the table to show all data, and formats it as an HTML
table.*/
function read($controller)
{
        $this->load->library('table');
        $tmpl = array (
                'table_open'            => '<table border="1"
cellpadding="4" cellspacing="0" width="100%">',
                'row_alt_start'         => '<tr bgcolor="grey">',
            );

        $this->table->set_template($tmpl);
        $this->load->database();
        $this->load->library('table');
        $query = $this->db->get($controller);
```

```
$result =   $this->table->generate($query);
$data['text'] = $result;
$this->display->mainpage($data);
}
```

The two highlighted lines do all the work of querying the database and formatting the results.

I've used the `mainpage` function in the `display` class to provide formatting for the page: the `read` function here just builds the data and hands it on as part of an array.

The result is a page full of data from the test file:

26	TestSite3	http://www.example3.com	alfred	albert	1	1	1	1	1	1	/files
24	TestSite1	http://www.example1.com	fred	bert	1	1	1	1	1	1	htdocs
25	Testsite2	http://www.example2.com	bert	fred	1	1	1	1	1	1	public_html
27	TestSite4	http://www.example4.com	alphonse	aloysius	1	1	1	1	1	1	

Let's just remind ourselves how control passes between the controller, the CRUD model, and other parts of the program.

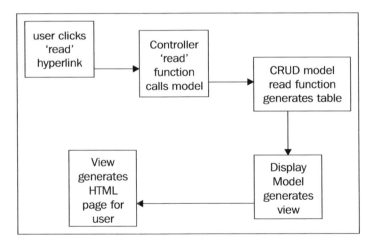

Delete and Trydelete

Deleting is the most permanent operation! For this reason our delete function checks to make sure of two things:

1. That a state variable of 'yes' has been set in the 'submit' field: if not, it passes the request to a `trydelete` function. That asks the user if she or he really does want to do a delete. If she or he confirms, the `trydelete` function sets a state variable of 'yes' and sends the request back to the delete function, which now accepts the delete instruction.

2. Before doing the delete query, it checks that an ID number has been set (otherwise all the entries might be deleted). Then, it uses CI's Active Record to do the delete and to check that one line has indeed been removed from the table. If one line was removed, then it returns to the `showall` function. You'll notice that it passes back two parameters—the controller name, and a message reporting that the deletion has been successfully done. (This is the second parameter to `showall`. If it is set, it appears in a red box at the top of the table, letting the user know what is going on.)

First, here's the delete function. You'll notice this code is also complicated by a lot of 'test block' lines. Ignore these for now: just follow the highlighted code..

```
/*DELETE FUNCTION: given table name and id number, deletes an entry*/
    function delete($controller, $idno, $state='no', $test='no')
            {
/*first check that the 'yes' flag is set. If not, go through the
trydelete function to give them a chance to change their minds*/
            if(!isset($state) || $state != 'yes')
                {
/*test block: are 'yes' flags recognised?*/
                    if($test == 'yes')
                    {
                            $place =   __FILE__.__LINE__;
                            $outcome = "exception at $place: sent state
value $state to trydelete function ";
                            return $outcome;
                    }
                    else
/*end test block*/
                        {$this->trydelete($controller, $idno, 'no');}
                }
            else{
/*'yes' flag is set, so now make sure there is an id number*/
            if(isset($idno) && $idno > 0 && is_int($idno))
/*test block: with this id no, am I going to do a delete?*/
                    {
                    if($test == 'yes')
                    {
                            $place =   __FILE__.__LINE__;
                            $outcome = "OK at $place:
                                doing delete on id of $idno ";
```

```
                    return $outcome;
                    }
            else{
/*end test block*/
/*if there is an id number, do the delete*/
                    $this->db->where('id', $idno);
                    $this->db->delete($controller);
                    $changes = $this->db->affected_rows();
                    }
            if($changes != 1)
                {
/*test block: did I actually do a delete? */
                    $place =   __FILE__ . __LINE__;
                    $outcome = "exception at $place: cdnt do delete
op on $controller with id no of $idno";
                    if($test == 'yes')
                            {return $outcome;}
                    else
/*end test block*/
/*if there was no update, report it*/
                                {$this->failure($outcome);}
                }
            else{
/*test block: I did do a delete*/
                    if($test == 'yes')
                        {return 'OK';}
                    else{
/*end test block: report the delete*/
                    $this->showall($controller,
                                "Entry no. $idno deleted.");}
                    }
                }
        else
 /*test block: report id number wasn't acceptable'*/
                {
                $place =   __FILE__ . __LINE__;
                $outcome = "exception at: $place : id no of $idno set
for delete op in $controller, expecting integer";
                    if($test == 'yes')
                        {return $outcome;}
                    else
/*endtest block: if I failed, report me*/
                            {$this->failure($outcome);}
                }
            }
    }
```

I promised to explain the $message parameter we used when we call showall. You can see it here: if this function is successful, it returns to the showall page, by calling it with an appropriate message:

```
$this->showall($controller, "Entry no. $idno deleted.");}
```

It's important not only that the action is done, but that the user knows it has been.

Now, back to preventing accidental deletions. If the delete function wasn't called with the state=yes parameter, it reroutes the request to the trydelete function—the 'second chance'. Actually, only the trydelete function will ever set this parameter to yes, so the delete form will always present an **are you sure** option to the user.

Let's look at the trydelete function. It creates a simple form, which looks like this:

> ## Are you sure you want to delete this entry?
> `[ yes ]`
> ## No, don't delete

Clicking on **yes** re-calls the delete function. (Notice again that the form can't return directly to crud/delete, because a form can't point to a model. It has to point to the sites/delete function in the controller, which simply passes everything straight on to the crud/delete function in the model again.)

The subtle change is that, if the user confirms the delete, the trydelete form adds (as a hidden field) the submit=yes parameter, which goes into the post array, and is returned to the controller's delete function. The controller's delete function reads the submit=yes parameter from the post array, and puts together a call to the crud/ delete function, which this time includes state=yes as a parameter, so the delete function moves on to the next step.

If the user doesn't want to do the delete, she or he clicks on the hyperlink created by the CI anchor function, and is passed back to the showall function, which is most probably where she or he came from.

Here's the code that does all this:

```
/*TRYDELETE FUNCION: interrupts deletes with an 'are you sure?
screen'*/
    function trydelete($controller, $idno, $submit = 'no')
            {
            if($state == 'yes')
                    {$this->delete($controller, $idno, 'yes');}
```

```
                else{
                        $result .= "<table><tr><td>Are you sure you want to
    delete this entry?</td></tr>";
                        $result .= form_open("$controller/delete");
                        $result .= form_hidden('id', $idno);
                        $result .= "<tr><td>";
                        $result .= form_submit('submit', 'yes');
                        $result .= "</td></tr>";
                        $result .= form_close();
                        $result .= "</table>";
                        $result .=   anchor("$controller/showall",
                                    "No, don't delete");
                        $data['text'] = $result;
                        $this->display->mainpage($data);
                        }
                }
```

Just for clarity, here's a diagram of how control passes during a delete operation.

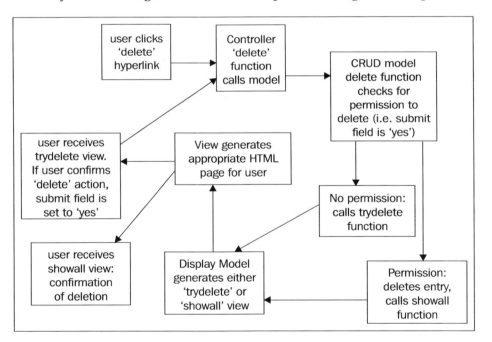

As you can see, this is quite complex, more so than our previous example. The model is doing all the work, but the user can only talk to the controller, so if you need to go back and re-present the question to the user, you need to involve the controller again.

However, once you've sorted it out, it works well and is highly logical. CI imposes this framework on you, but in the long run that's an advantage. Your code is consistent, and modular. Note how the same `display` model and the same view is invoked each time: what they show the user depends on the CRUD model function that called them.

Insert

This is the most complex function, because it generates a form for users to fill out. (Interface with humans is always the most difficult thing…)

Rather than write two separate functions, one to insert and one to update, and have to build the form twice, I've written one function that does duty for both. If you supply a valid ID number, it updates the corresponding record; if not, it inserts a new entry.

To make this easier to follow, I haven't included the test blocks that we saw in the delete function.

This is where we use the array we defined at the beginning of this chapter. The function sets up a form, using CI's form helper, and based on the type of form element we specified in the array (dropdown, textarea, etc.). At the heart of the function is a switch statement, which accomplishes this.

The code uses CI's validation class to help us check the incoming data: remember we set the validation rules in our initial array.

```
/*the most complex function. This creates an HTML form, based on the
description of the fields in the form array. This is sent to our
display model, which sets up a view and shows it to the user.
The view then sends a POST array back to the controller. The form
can't call this model directly, so it has to call the controller,
which refers it back to the model.
Note the function parameters:
1. The controller parameter is whichever controller/ table has called
the model - eg the 'sites' controller, or the 'domains' controller.
The controller has the same name as the table it manipulates.
2. The optional id parameter is the id of an individual entry in that
table.
3. The optional 'test' parameter is so you can set the form up to make
usable responses to self-test functions.
*/
    function insert($controller='', $id=0, $test='no')
    {
        $myform = '';
        $myid = 0;
```

```
                    $currentvalue = array();
/*test if the table exists*/
        if(!$this->db->table_exists($controller))
            {
              $place =   __FILE__.__LINE__;
              $outcome = "exception: $place:looking for table
$controller: it doesn't exist'";
                if($test =='yes')
                    {
                     return $outcome;
                    }
            else{
              $this->failure($outcome, $controller);
                    }
            }
        else
        {
                          if($test =='yes')
                          {
                          return 'OK';
                          }
        }
/*end test block*/

/*next check if there is an id number. If there is, we need to get the
values to populate the table fields*/
        if(isset($id) && $id > 0)
            {$myid = $id;
            $this->db->where('id', $id);
            $query = $this->db->get($controller);
            if ($query->num_rows() > 0)
                {
                $row = $query->row();
//-------------work out the values we want!
                foreach($row as $key =>$value)
/*
first of all work out what value you want to show as the existing
value in each line of the form. In priority order these are:
1. the last value the user entered, from the post array
2. the value from the database
3. nothing, if neither of these is set.
if we got here, the id does exist and is returning values, so get the
existing values into a value array. Or, if there is something in the
validation array, use that instead*/
                {
                $_POST[$key] = $this->validation->$key;
```

```
                    if(isset($_POST[$key]))
                            {$currentvalue[$key] = $_POST[$key];}
                    else
                            {$currentvalue[$key] = $value;}
                    }
/*test block: there was an id number, so has the program gone for an
update? if this is not a test, of course, just do the update*/
                    if($test == 'yes')
                            {
                            $place =   __FILE__ . __LINE__ ;
                            $outcome = "exception: $place: id of $id
returned results from $controller table so have gone for update";
                            return $outcome;
                            }

/*end test block*/
                            $myform .= "<tr><td colspan='2'>Update
existing entry number $id</td></tr>";
                            }
/*now catch situation where this query isn't returning results. We
could only have got here with an integer set as our ID number, so
this probably means we are trying to delete an entry that doesn't
exist.*/
                    else{
                            $place =   __FILE__ . __LINE__ ;
                            $outcome = "exception: $place: despite
id of $id cant get any results from $controller table";
                    if($test == 'yes')
/*test block: there was and ID but there were no results*/
                            {
                            return $outcome;
                            }
/*end test block*/
                    else
                            {$this->failure($outcome, $controller);}
                            }
                    }
/*there was no ID number, so this is a new entry*/
            else{
/*If the user has filled in values, and has returned here because some
of them didn't validate, we still need to repopulate the form with
what he entered, so he only has to alter the one that didn't validate.
Get these from the post array*/
                    if(isset($_POST))
                            {
                            foreach($_POST as $key => $value)
```

```
                                    {
                                     if(isset($_POST[$key]))
                                       {$currentvalue[$key] = $_POST[$key];}
                                    }

                         }
               $myform .= "<tr><td colspan='2'>New entry</td></tr>";

/*test block: there was no ID, so this is a new entry*/
                         if($test == 'yes')
                              {
                              $place =   __FILE__.__LINE__;
                              $outcome = "exception: $place: id of $id
treated as no id, so going for new entry";
                              return $outcome;
                              }
/*end test block*/
                    }

/*the table exists, whether this is an update or new entry, so start
to build the form*/
          $myform      .=      "<table class='table'>";
          $myform .= form_open("$controller/interim");
          $myform .= '<p>This entry could not be made because...</P>';
          $myform .= $this->validation->error_string;


/*the rest of this function is common to inserts or update.
Look up in the form array which form field type you want to display,
and then build up the html for each different type, as well as
inserting the values you want it to echo.*/


                    foreach($this->form[$controller] as $key => $value)
                    {
/*This switch statement develops several types of HTML form field
based on information in the form array.
It doesn't yet cover checkboxes or radio or password fields. It adds
a 'readonly' type, which is a field that only displays a value and
doesn't let the user modify it*/

                    $fieldtype = $value[1];
                    $val_string = $this->validation->$key;
                    switch($value[1])
                         {
/*a simple input line*/
                         case 'input':
                         $data = array(
                    'name'          => $key,
```

```
            'id'            => $key,
            'value'         => $currentvalue[$key],
            'maxlength'     => '100',
            'size'          => '50',
            'style'         => 'width:50%',
        );
                $myform .= "<tr><td>$value[0]</td><td>";
                $myform .= form_input($data);
                $myform .= "</td></tr>";
                if($test == 'second')
                        {
                        return 'input';
                        }
                break;

                case 'textarea':
/*a text area field.*/
                $data = array(
            'name'          => $key,
            'id'            => $key,
            'value'         => $currentvalue[$key],
            'rows'          => '6',
            'cols'          => '70',
            'style'         => 'width:50%',
        );
                $myform .= "<tr><td valign=
                                    'top'>$value[0]</td><td>";
                $myform .= form_textarea($data);
                $myform .= "</td></tr>";
                break;

                case 'dropdown':
/*a drop-down box. Values are dynamically generated from whichever
table was specified in the forms array. This table must have an id
field (which is now entered in the form) and a name field (which is
displayed in the drop-down box).*/
                $dropbox = array();
                if(isset($value[3]))
                        {
                        $temptable = $value[3];
                        $this->db->select('id, name');
                        $query = $this->db->get($temptable);
                        if ($query->num_rows() > 0)
                            {
                            foreach ($query->result() as $row)
                            {
                             $dropbox[$row->id] = $row->name;
                            }
                            }
                }
```

```
                              $myform .= "<tr><td valign=
                                              'top'>$value[0]</td><td>";
                              $myform .= form_dropdown($key, $dropbox,
$currentvalue[$key]);
                              $myform .= "</td></tr>";
                              break;

                              case 'submit':
/*a submit field*/
                              $myform .= "<tr><td>$value[0]</td><td>";
                              $time  =  time();
                              $data = array(
                'name'           => 'submit',
                'id'             => 'submit',
            );
                              $myform .= form_submit($data);
                              $myform .= "</td></tr>";

                              break;

                              case 'hidden':
/*generates a hidden field*/
                              $myform .= form_hidden($key,
$currentvalue[$key]);
                              break;

                              case 'readonly':
/*generates a field the user can see, but not alter.*/

                              $myform .= "<tr><td>$value[0]</td><td>$current
value[$key]";

                              $myform .= form_hidden($key,
$currentvalue[$key]);
                              $myform .= "</td></tr>";

                              break;

                              case 'timestamp':
/*generates a timestamp the first time it's set*/
//                            $myform .= "<tr><td>$value[0]</td><td>now()";
                              $timenow = time();

    if($currentvalue[$key]==''||$currentvalue[$key]==0)
                              {$time = $timenow;}
                              else{$time = $currentvalue[$key];}
                              $myform .= form_hidden($key, $time);
                              $myform .= "</td></tr>";

                              break;

                              case 'updatestamp':
/*generates a timestamp each time it's altered or viewed*/
//                            $myform .= "<tr><td>$value[0]</td><td>now()";
```

```
                    $timenow = time();
                    $myform .= form_hidden($key, $timenow);
                    $myform .= "</td></tr>";

                    break;

                    default:
                    $place =    __FILE__ . __LINE__ ;
                    $outcome = "exception: $place:
                                    switch can't handle $fieldtype";
/*test block: what if the switch doesn't recognise the form type?'*/
                    if($test == 'second')
                        {
                        return $outcome;
                        }
/*test block ends*/
                    else {

                    $this->failure($outcome, $controller);
                        }
                    }
/*end the foreach loop which generates the form*/
                }
                $myform .= form_hidden('submit',$time);
                $myform .= form_close();
                $myform .= "</table>";

/*Finally we've built our form and populated it! Now, stuff the form
in an array variable and send it to the model which builds up the rest
of the view.*/
                $data['text'] = $myform;
                $this->display->mainpage($data);
    }
```

A couple of things to explain here. All the form field types are standard, except for
readonly—which is a hidden form field that allows you to see, but not to alter, what
it says. This is not secure, of course: a smart user can easily hack the value. It's just
designed to simplify the choices the user faces.

You'll notice the form points to a function called interim, on whichever controller
called it. Again, that's because you can't address a model directly via its URL. So, if
it was set up by the 'sites' controller, the form points to 'sites/interim' and the values
entered by the user, or from existing data, are packed in the $_POST array and sent
there. As you'll recall from the beginning of this chapter, that function just calls the
crud function insert2, passing on the $_POST array to it as a parameter.

Insert2

Insert2 receives the $_POST array as a parameter and checks to see if it has an 'id' field set. If yes, it updates that entry. If not, it creates a new entry.

In order that CI's validation class, which requires a $_POST array, can work, our function renames the array it received as a parameter as $_POST.

```
function insert2($controller, $newpost, $test = 'no')
        {
        $myform = '';

/*test the incoming parameters*/
        if(!$this->db->table_exists($controller))
        {
//test here!
        }


        $this->load->library('validation');

/*handle the validation. Note that the validation class works from
the post array, whereas this function only has a $newpost array: same
data, but different name. So we re-create the $_POST array.
*/
        $_POST = $newpost;

/*now build up the validation rules from the entries in our master
array*/
        $errorform = '';
        $newtemparray = $this->form[$controller];
        foreach($newtemparray as $key => $value)
            {$rules[$key]= $value[2];}
        $this->validation->set_rules($rules);

/*and the name fields*/
        foreach($newtemparray as $key => $value)
            {$fields[$key]= $value[0];}
        $this->validation->set_fields($fields);


    $this->validation->set_fields($fields);

/*now do the validation run*/
        if ($this->validation->run() == FALSE)
                {
/*if the validation run fails, re-present the entry form by calling
the 'insert' function*/
                $id = $_POST['id'];
                $this->insert($controller, $id, 'no', $_POST);
```

```
                    }
            else
            {
/*The validation check was OK so we carry on. Check if there is an id
number*/
            if(isset($_POST['id']) && $_POST['id'] > 0)
                {
/*if yes: this is an update, so you don't want the id number in the
post array because it will confuse the autoincrement id field in the
database. Remove it, but save it in $tempid to use in the 'where'
condition of the update query, then do the update*/
                $tempid = $_POST['id'];
                unset($_POST['id']);
                $this->db->where('id', $tempid);
                $this->db->update($controller, $_POST);
                if($this->db->affected_rows()== 1)
                    {$this->showall($controller, "Entry number
$tempid updated.");}
                else{$this->failure("Failed to update $controller for
id no $tempid", __FILE__,__LINE__);}

/*if no id number, we assume this is a new entry: no need to unset the
post array id as it isn't there! the database will create its own id
number. Do the new entry*/
                $this->db->insert($controller, $_POST);
                if($this->db->affected_rows()== 1)
                    {$this->showall($controller,
                                    "New entry added.");}
                else{$this->failure("Failed to make new entry in
$controller ", __FILE__,__LINE__);}
                }
                }
            }
```

And that's it. A few hundred lines of code, which allow you to do CRUD on any table.

The Test Suite

Remember those 'test blocks' in the delete function? Their purpose is simply to detect if the function is being run 'for real' or for a test, and, if the latter, to make sure that it returns a value we can easily test.

This is all because, at the end of the CRUD model, we have a 'self-test' suite. This is called by the test function in any controller (it doesn't matter which one) and performs generalized CRUD tests using a dummy table.

First in the CRUD class there is a master 'test' function, which only exists to call the others.

```
/*now a suite of self-test functions.*/

/*first function just calls all the others and supplies any formatting
you want. Also it builds/ destroys temporary data table before/ after
tests on the database.*/
    function test()
        {
        $return = "<h3>Test results</h3>";
        $this->extendarray();
        $return .= $this->testarray();
        $this->reducearray();
        $return .= $this->testarray();
        $this->testbuild();
        $return .= $this->testdelete();
        $this->testdestroy();
        $return .= $this->testinsert();
        $return .= $this->testinsert2();
        $return .= $this->testshowall();
        $data['text'] = $return;
        $this->display->mainpage($data);
        }
```

This just assembles any tests you want, and runs them.

However, rather than go through all these functions, let's just show one: the test function called `testdelete()`.

First, though, we need two functions: one to build, and one to destroy, our special dummy testing table, 'fred'. The first function destroys any existing 'fred' table, builds another, and puts a line of test data in it:

```
/*this function builds a new temporary table. 'fred', in your database
so you can test the CRUD functions on it without losing real data*/
    function testbuild()
    {
      $this->db->query("DROP TABLE IF EXISTS fred");
      $this->db->query("CREATE TABLE IF NOT EXISTS fred (id INT(11)
default NULL, name varchar(12) default NULL)");
      $this->db->query("INSERT INTO fred VALUES (1, 'bloggs')");
    }
```

Depending on the test you want to run, you can make this more elaborate—e.g., populate more fields, or have more rows of data.

The second destroys the table so we can start afresh. There ought not to be any value left in it after we've done the delete test, but in case that failed, or in case we write other tests, let's make sure:

```
/*this function destroys the temporary table, to avoid any confusion
later on*/
    function testdestroy()
    {
      $this->db->query("DROP TABLE IF EXISTS fred");
    }
```

Now we can start to test the delete function:

```
    function testdelete()
    {
    $result = '<p>Deletion test</p>';
```

The first test we might do is to make sure that the 'delete' function intercepts any delete call without a $state parameter of yes, and sends it to the trydelete function to ask 'are you sure?'

Remember that we want the test to return 'OK' if the program handles each possibility correctly—not if the possibility itself is 'right' or 'wrong'. So if the 'state' parameter says 'haggis', which is clearly 'wrong', the test should say 'OK' as long as the program treats it as 'not yes'! Ideally, we only want a short list highlighting the failures: if the tests are successful, we don't need to know the details.

First we set up an array, in which each key is an expression we might use in a test, and the corresponding value is the result we expect:

```
    $states = array(
                    'no'    =>      'exception',
                    '1'     =>      'exception',
                    'haggis'=>      'exception',
                    'yyyes' =>      'exception',
                    'yes'   =>      'OK'
                    );
    foreach($states AS $testkey => $testvalue)
          {$test = $this->delete('fred', 1, $testkey, 'yes');
 /*if you got the value you want, preg_match returns 1*/
          $result .=  $this->unit->run(preg_match("/$testvalue/",
 $test), 1, $test);
          }
```

Assuming our code is working properly, that will return:

Test Name	exception at E:\xampplite\htdocs\packt2\system\application\models\crud.php657: sent state value no to trydelete function
Test Datatype	Integer
Expected Datatype	Integer
Result	Passed
File Name	E:\xampplite\htdocs\packt2\system\application\models\crud.php
Line Number	876

Test Name	exception at E:\xampplite\htdocs\packt2\system\application\models\crud.php657: sent state value 1 to trydelete function
Test Datatype	Integer
Expected Datatype	Integer
Result	Passed
File Name	E:\xampplite\htdocs\packt2\system\application\models\crud.php
Line Number	876

Test Name	exception at E:\xampplite\htdocs\packt2\system\application\models\crud.php657: sent state value yyyes to trydelete function
Test Datatype	Integer
Expected Datatype	Integer
Result	Passed
File Name	E:\xampplite\htdocs\packt2\system\application\models\crud.php
Line Number	876

Our next test is to see how, given a correct state, the delete function reacts to a series of ID values—including non-integers, negative values, etc. Be careful about the granularity of the tests. For instance 9999 is a valid ID number in that it is an integer and greater than 0, but it won't lead to a delete operation as we only have one record, with an ID of 1! You need to be clear which stage of the process you are testing.

```
/*given $state set to 'yes', test another array of values for the id
number. Start by building a test table*/
   $this->testbuild();
/*then another array of values to test, and the results you expect..*/
   $numbers = array(
              '9999' =>     'OK',
              '-1'   =>     'exception',
              'NULL' =>     'exception',
              '0'    =>     'exception',
              '3.5'  =>     'exception',
              ''     =>     'exception',
              '1'    =>     'OK'
              );
```

```
/*now do the tests*/
    foreach($numbers AS $testkey => $testvalue)
            {$test = $this->delete('fred', $testkey, 'yes', 'yes');
         $result         .=      $this->unit->run(preg_match("/
$testvalue/", $test), 1, $test);
            }
/*destroy the test table, just in case*/
    $this->testdestroy();
/*return the results of this test*/
    return $result;
    }
```

All being well, that will return something like this:

Test Name	OK at E:\xampplite\htdocs\packt2\system\application\models\crud.php675: doing delete on id of 1
Test Datatype	Integer
Expected Datatype	Integer
Result	Passed
File Name	E:\xampplite\htdocs\packt2\system\application\models\crud.php
Line Number	876

Test Name	exception at: E:\xampplite\htdocs\packt2\system\application\models\crud.php708 : id no of 3.5 set for delete op in fred, expecting integer
Test Datatype	Integer
Expected Datatype	Integer
Result	Passed
File Name	E:\xampplite\htdocs\packt2\system\application\models\crud.php
Line Number	901

Test Name	exception at: E:\xampplite\htdocs\packt2\system\application\models\crud.php708 : id no of set for delete op in fred, expecting integer
Test Datatype	Integer
Expected Datatype	Integer
Result	Passed
File Name	E:\xampplite\htdocs\packt2\system\application\models\crud.php
Line Number	901

You can add as many tests as you wish.

Testing helps the development process. As you think about different values to put in your test arrays, you have to consider whether your code will in fact handle them gracefully.

It may also help later on, if you change your code and accidentally introduce errors; and it will reassure you, once the code goes to a production site, to run a test now and then.

Summary

This has been a long chapter but it has drawn a lot together. We've seen:

- How to generalize CRUD operations so that you can do them with two classes: one for the controller, and one for the CRUD model. The former needs to be repeated for each table, the latter stays the same.

- As a result we could built in various checks and safeguards, as well as tests, so we can be confident that our CRUD operations are done.

Using CI has allowed us to write all of this in a few hundred lines of (relatively) simple code, which we can reuse on almost any site we build, provided we obey a few simple naming and layout rules. To me, that's what frameworks are all about.

14
The Verdict on CI

This book started out with some specific examples of how CodeIgniter can save you time and effort when you are writing websites using PHP. We've gone through some of the many things CI can do, using as a basis some parts of a website that will conduct regular tests of other websites. I hope that these examples have shown how CI makes coding much easier at the macro level.

In this chapter, I'd like to step back a little and look at the overall impact of using the CodeIgniter framework. Does it make writing a complete application easier? Can it produce professional results?

When you write a book like this, it's important to divide it up into sections and focus on one new trick at a time. That means that it's sometimes difficult to see how all the bits fit together. I hope the 'Instant CRUD' code in the last chapter went some way to putting different bits of code together, mixing up Active Record and unit testing and forms. In this chapter, I'd like to show how all the pieces can fit together to deliver a finished project. In other words, does our website-testing project work?

Taking this top-down look at some specimen code from the site should help us to draw up a balance sheet:

- Where CI helped
    1. Organizing the site
    2. Making the code simpler
    3. Doing things for you (data validation etc.)
- Where CI wasn't of much help.

Some Code: the 'do_test' Model

What follows is a detailed look at part of one model on our site. This model works from the 'tests' table and the 'events' table. Its purpose is to control the most central function of our site i.e. the tests that it does on remote sites. This model:

- Links the database tables listing the sites and the tests
- Updates another table, which lists events (i.e., each time a test is carried out)
- Helps interface with the user, allowing him or her to select a test pattern or to get information in various formats

Because it's a model, it needs to be called by a controller, and it returns its results to a view. If the view contains hyperlinks, these in turn call a controller function, which acts as a 'front end' for another model function.

Here's one of the do_test model's main functions, to generate a table of information directly from a database query. The idea is to list the sites available and select one to be tested. If you haven't selected one already, the function generates a list of sites and asks you to choose. The code looks like this:

```
/*this function prepares a report on existing tests and allows you to
choose which to do.
  First, it selects a site and reports on that*/
    function report($site=0,$message='')
    {
/*have you chosen a site yet?*/
    $siteid = $this->uri->segment(3, 0);
    if(!$siteid > 0)
        {
        $text = "<table class='table'>";
        $text .=    "<tr><td colspan = '2'>Select a site to work
                    on</td></tr><tr>";
        $this->db->select('name, id');
        $query = $this->db->get('sites');
        if ($query->num_rows() > 0)
            {
            foreach ($query->result() as $row)
                {
                $text .=        "<tr><td>";
            $text .=        $row->name;
                $text .=        "</td><td>";
/*note the next line uses the CI anchor function to generate
hyperlinks*/
                $text .=        anchor("tests/report/$row->id","Select");
                $text .=        "</td></tr>";
```

```
                                }
                        }
                $response['mytext'] = $text;
                $response['message']= $message;
                $this->display->mainpage($response);
        }
```

The result, when it's called via a controller, looks like this:

Run tests Sites Domains People Hosts Tests Events Frequencies XMLRPC Logout	
Select a site to work on	
ATestSite1	Select
ATestSite2	Select
ATestSite3	Select
ATestSite4	Select
ATestSite5	Select

Notice there's a hyperlink for each option, so you can select that site. I'd have liked to use the HTML 'Table' class to do this automatically, but I can't see an easy way to include hyperlinks in the result rows if I do. But:

- CI's active record class makes the database queries much easier to write
- CI's anchor function (part of the URL helper) makes it easier to write the hyperlinks

And, of course, when we come to move our site from my development server to the web, we know that these two CI functions will ensure that the database connection information, and the site configuration details such as the URL, are automatically changed.

CI helped me to organize the code, too. The $siteid variable is passed in as part of a URI segment when the model is called from the menu.

Notice how the actual web page is created via the mainpage function of the display model. All the do_test model has to do is take the specific information we need out of the database, and send it off. The display model ensures that it is formatted according to our .css file, and laid out on a page with a menu bar, etc.

I'm not being quite proper here, of course, since the table formatting is in the dotest model. There are far too many angle brackets in there: ideally, they should be in a view file. However, this would have required us to design a 'view' file specially for this piece of data. It seemed simpler to do it this way. At least the design information is kept out of the way in the .css file.

Now we move on to the next part of this function. If you have selected a site, the view now lets us see the tests that have been done for that particular site.

The code looks like this—it's the `else` loop following the:

```
if(!$siteid > 0)
```

In other words, this is what happens if a valid `$siteid` was passed.

```
        else
        {
/*ok, you've chosen a site. let's go to town*/
    $this->db->select('sites.name AS sitename, sites.url AS siteurl,
tests.name AS testname, tests.lastdone AS lastdone, tests.id AS
testid, frequency, sites.id AS siteid, tests.type AS type');
    $this->db->join('sites', 'sites.id = tests.siteid');
    $this->db->orderby('frequency desc, sitename asc');
    $this->db->where('sites.id', $siteid);
    $query = $this->db->get('tests');
    if ($query->num_rows() > 0)
    {
    $xrow        = $query->row();
    $report = "<table class='table'><tr ><td colspan='4'>Test report on
$xrow->sitename</td></tr>";
    $report .= "<tr class='header'><td width ='25%'>Test</td><td
width ='15%'>Type</td><td width ='10%'>Frequency</td><td width
='40%'>Result</td></tr>";
            foreach ($query->result() as $row)
            {
            $report .= "<tr><td width ='25%'>";
            $report .= $row->testname;
            $report .= "</td><td width ='15%'>";
            $report .= $row->type;
            $report .= "</td><td width ='10%'>";
//          $report .= $row->lastdone;
            $this->db->select('name');
            $this->db->where('id', $row->frequency);
            $fquery = $this->db->get('frequencies');
            if ($fquery->num_rows() > 0)
                {
                $frow = $fquery->row();
                $sid = $frow->name;
                }
            $report .= $sid;
            $report .= "</td><td width ='40%'>";
            $alf =  $this->deadline($row->testid);
            if($alf== FALSE)
                {$report .= "Overdue: ";
```

```
                          $report .= anchor("tests/runtest/$row->testid/human",
                                                          'do it now');}
              else{$report .= "Last done: $alf";}
              $report .= "</td></tr>";
              }
     $report .= "<tr><td colspan='4'>";
     $report .= anchor("tests/runalltests/$row->siteid", 'run all
outstanding tests now');
     $report .= "</table>";
     }
     else
     $report = "no tests for this site yet.";}
     $report .="<table class='table'><tr class='header'><td>Other
options</td></tr>";
     $report .= "<tr><td>";
     $report .= anchor("tests/getwrittenreport/$row->siteid/604800",
'Get a written report for last week');
     $report .= anchor("tests/getwrittenreport/$row->siteid/2592000",
'Get a written report for last month');
          $report .= "</tr><tr><td>";
     $report .= anchor("tests/getbaseremotefiles/$row->siteid", 'Update
remote file list for this site');
          $report .= "</td></tr><table>";
     $response['mytext'] = $report;
$this->display->mainpage($response);
     }
}
```

The result of this code looks like this:

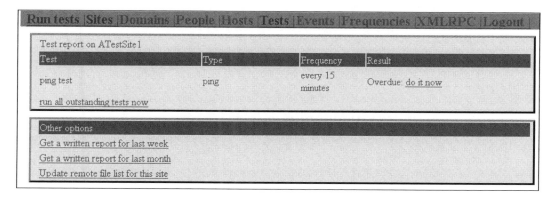

You can see that it has consulted the database to find out which tests should be applied to our selected site. There's only one test, a simple 'ping' which is supposed to be done every 15 minutes.

It hasn't been done in the last 15 minutes, so it's shown as overdue and a hyperlink allows me to do it now if I want to. If I click on the hyperlink, I call the tests controller's `runtest` function, supplying it with the ID number of the test I want.

The result looks like this:

| Run tests | Sites | Domains | People | Hosts | Tests | Events | Frequencies | XMLRPC | Logout |

Test took 0.1942.			Result was OK

Statistics for this test

Data for: ping test

Time	Problem?	Time taken	Result, if not successful
18 Apr 2007 15 52	n	0.1942	

The system tells me when the test has been done, that there was no problem with it, and how long it took.

If I now go back to the `report` function, you'll recall that there were options to generate historical reports on tests conducted on my selected site over the last week or the last month. I've only set this site up as an example, so it has no real test history: but this is how it looks if I do a series of identical tests in quick succession. I've also added another test, and the report includes that as well.

| Run tests | Sites | Domains | People | Hosts | Tests | Events | Frequencies | XMLRPC | Logout |

Site name: ATestSite1

- Location: http://www.example1.com.
- Client is 1
- Report at 18:4:2007 16:46

Tests on this site are:

Name	Last done	Last status
ping test	18:4:2007 16:36	OK
check front page content	18:4:2007 16:45	OK

Test history:

Time	Done	Time taken	Status
18:4:2007 16:45	check front page content	0.1625	OK
18:4:2007 16:36	ping test	0.1592	OK
18:4:2007 16:36	ping test	0.1578	OK
18:4:2007 16:35	ping test	0.167	OK
18:4:2007 16:35	ping test	0.1775	OK

As you can see, we're building up a report that we could show to a client, to demonstrate that the site was alive and responding when it was tested in different ways at various times. The time taken for each test to respond is not of much interest at any one time, but may help us to see a pattern over a longer period.

The function that actually runs the tests is built around a `switch` statement. It takes two parameters:

- The ID number of the test, from which we look up basic information that we need to run it: the URL to use, any name/value pairs, and any text we expect to find if the test is successful.

- The type of user. (If the user is 'human', the programme returns more information in a more user-friendly format—in other words, if you want to display the result on a screen, call it with the user parameter set to human. If you want to handle the results programmatically, set this parameter to something else.)

In this excerpt from the code, we've defined several types of test. Two examples are:

- 'ping' tests which simply call the URL. If they get a result, they examine it either for an expected phrase (called 'regex' in the database) or for a generic HTML term if there is no 'regex' phrase set.

- 'ete' tests which use some code we developed to make an 'end-to-end' test of a protected page, logging in and looking for an expected phrase. This code is not explained in this book as its not included in CI's functionality.

Each test returns a `$result` and a `$timetaken` variable; these are entered into the 'events' table of the database as a record of the test, together with the other information from the database. Here's the code, which draws heavily on the CI Active Record model to read from and write to the database, and on the benchmark class to get the times taken by each test.

```
/*function to run an individual test*/
    function runtest($testid, $user='human')
    {
/*first, look up the test details */
    $this->db->where('id', $testid);
    $query = $this->db->get('tests');
    if ($query->num_rows() > 0)
            {
    foreach ($query->result() as $row)
                {
                    $type = $row->type;
/*then work out which type it is and forward it accordingly*/
```

```
                    switch ($type){
                    case 'ping':
                    $this->benchmark->mark('code_start');
                    $result =$this->pingtest($testid);
                    $this->benchmark->mark('code_end');
                    $timetaken = $this->benchmark->elapsed_time('code_
start', 'code_end');
                break;

                    case 'ete' :
                    $this->benchmark->mark('code_start');
                    $result = $this->httppost($testid);
                    $this->benchmark->mark('code_end');
                    $timetaken = $this->benchmark->elapsed_time('code_
start', 'code_end');
                    break;

                    default:
                    $result = 'noid';
                    }
/*work out which site the test belongs to*/
                    $this->db->select('tests.siteid AS id');
                    $this->db->where('id', $testid);
                    $query = $this->db->get('tests');
                    if ($query->num_rows() > 0)
                        {$srow = $query->row();
                        $mysiteid = $srow->id;
                        }
                    else{$mysiteid = 0;}

/*build the rest of the result set and enter it into the database*/
                    $time = now();

                    if($result == 'OK')
                        {$isalert = 'n';}
                    else{$isalert = 'y';}

                    $this->db->set('name', $type);
                    $this->db->set('type', 'test');
                    $this->db->set('timetaken', $timetaken);
                    if($result != '')
                    {$this->db->set('result', $result);}
                    $this->db->set('testid', $testid);
                    $this->db->set('userid', 0);
                    $this->db->set('siteid', $mysiteid);
                    $this->db->set('time', $time);
```

```
            $this->db->set('isalert', $isalert);
            $this->db->insert('events');

        $mydata = array(
        'lastdone'        => $time,
        'notes'           => $result,
        'isalert'         => $isalert
    );
            $this->db->where('id', $testid);
            $this->db->update('tests', $mydata);
/*only return this info to screen if user is human. Otherwise, no need
to do anything more; you've updated the database.*/
            if($user == 'human')
                {$mytext = "<table class='table'><tr>";
                $mytext .= "<td>Test took $timetaken.</td>";
                $mytext .= "<td>Result was ".$result.
                                        '</td></tr></table>';
                $mytext .= $this->testhistory($testid);
                $response['mytext'] = $mytext;
                $this->display->mainpage($response);}
            else{return $response;}
                }
            }
        }
```

How we actually print out the test report is an interesting example of CI in action. As ever, there is a range of choices. You can print out your report the hard way, using HTML in your code as we did earlier, like this:

```
/*do database query here!*/
/*now format the results the hard way......*/

    $report .= "<p>Test history:</p>";
    $report .= "<table width='100%'><tr><td width ='20%'>Time</
td><td width ='20%'>Name</td><td width ='10%'>Time taken</td><td
width='45%'>Status</td></tr>";if ($query->num_rows() > 0)
            {
            foreach ($query->result() as $row)
                {
                $report .= "<tr><td width='20%'>";
                $report .= gmDate("j:n:Y H:i", $row->time);
                $report .= "</td><td width='20%'>";
                $report .= $row->name;
                $report .= "</td><td width=10%>";
                $report .= $row->timetaken;
```

```
        $report .= "</td><td width = 45%>";
        if($row->isalert == 'n')
                {$report .= "OK";}
        else
                {$report .= "problem: $row->result";}

        $report .= "</td></tr>";
        }
    $report .= "</table>";
```

On the other hand, you could use the HTML Table library to make life easier:

```
/*do db query here */
/*format the results using the CI HTML table library*/
    $report .= "Test history:";

/*redefine our CI table layout if we want to, using our css file*/
    $tmpl = array ('table_open'        => '<table border="1",
class="table">',);
    $this->table->set_template($tmpl);

    if ($query->num_rows() > 0)
            {
            $this->table->set_heading('Time of test', 'Name ,'Time
taken','Result');
            $report .= $this->table->generate($query3);
            }
            $this->table->clear();
```

Clearly, shorter and simpler. The results appear exactly the same, depending only on the HTML formatting. However, let's look at two issues that this code raises.

When you look more closely, there is a compromise that comes with convenience. In the first, longer, version, it is possible to format the date:

```
    $report .= gmDate("j:n:Y H:i", $row->time);
```

This gives me a 'human' date rather than the Unix date I've actually stored in my database. In other words, the table says '24 Apr 2007 09 04' rather than '1177405479'. However, it isn't easy to do this with the CI HTML Table functions. (You might be able to do this within the database query itself in some database systems; but MySQL's date functions only operate on dates and times stored in MySQL's unique date format, and we chose to use the Unix format instead.) We had the same trouble earlier on when we wanted to generate hyperlinks. You can't do it this way.

There's another big question about this. Where should the formatting go? All the code written previously should appear either in a controller or a model. (As I've written it, it's in a model, which is called by controllers when the human user clicks on a hyperlink to generate reports. The reason for putting it in a model is so I can call the code from several controllers if I need to.)

MVC purists would say that you should never put formatting in a model. It should be in a view. And, indeed, they've got a point. I might want to rewrite the code to produce a text report, and use CI's download helper to force the site to download it in text format rather than display it on the screen. (See Chapter 11 for more about the download helper.) As it is, I've got to re-write all the code to produce something formatted with text breaks rather than `<tr></tr>` pairs—or, even worse, to produce format in `.rtf`, or some similar rich-text format.

The other option is to use the alternative PHP syntax or the Template Parser class and put variables, or placeholders, actually in the views themselves. (See Chapter 5 for a brief coverage of these options.) Then, all you pass to the view is the actual data, unformatted. While this may satisfy the MVC purists, I find it adds an extra layer of complexity to the code. But this is a personal view, and many would disagree.

The main point is that CI offers a range of options: it's up to you to choose the one you are happiest with. There is no 'right' or 'wrong' way: there are just some ways that work better than others, and some ways that suit your personal style better than others.

A Balance Sheet

Let's look back over what we've covered in this book. Was CI helpful?

Where CI Helped: Structure

Even from looking at a part of just one model on our site, it's obvious that any worthwhile application quickly becomes complex. CI, by suggesting and to some extent enforcing an MVC structure, helps bring some order to that complexity. It's still possible to forget where you put a piece of code, or even write a similar function twice in different controllers or models: but it's more likely that your code will be in logical chunks.

CI's URL mechanism helps you quickly link from one code file to another.

CI's 'super-object' structure makes sure that the pieces of code can call each other and pass information around, without namespace conflicts. We are less likely to have confusions between variables with the same name, because each one is confined to its own area. At the same time, you can easily access all the CI resources on your site, from wherever you are in your code.

CI's 'config' files encourage you to build up a centralized collection of information about your site.

All these benefits mean that your site will be easier to develop, easier to maintain, and easier for other programmers to understand.

Where CI Helped: Simplicity

There are lots of places where CI helps simplify your code. Perhaps the best examples come from the Active Record class, but there are many others in this book. CI is excellent at taking complex chunks of code, hiding them away in a function of some library class, and allowing you to use them with a simple function call.

Where CI Helped: Extra Functionality

Many CI functions bring additional benefits when you use them. Functions like the URL class and Active Record automatically refer to your 'config' settings, so you don't have to keep repeating information, and so that any changes you make in one place are automatically applied across the site.

There are lots of small examples—the easy way you can hide your email addresses from robots, for example (see Chapter 3), or that the Active Record class also prepares your data.

In fact, one of the main learning curves (for me at least) with CI is finding out what shortcuts are available, and remembering to use them instead of writing it all out the laborious long-hand PHP way that I'm used to. If this book draws your attention to some of these shortcuts, it will have served a useful purpose for that alone.

Problems with CI

CI isn't perfect. This really means that it is a balancing act: lightness and ease of use against complexity and completeness. As somebody once said, 'lightweight' means, "includes everything I want and nothing that I don't want".

Completeness

CI contains functions for almost every regular application you can think of. There are some exceptions to the subjects covered by the main CI classes, and many of them are covered by additional libraries contributed by CI users (see the next chapter) or available through the PEAR repository. The most obvious omissions include:

- An AJAX class
- A class to write web robots
- A class to build a secure site, handling logging in, protected pages, and such like, as well as basic session maintenance
- An improved 'scaffolding' class, producing something that could be used on a public site rather than purely for development

CI might also take a leaf from the Rails book, and build a code generator class—which would allow developers to build self-customizing classes.

Ease of Use

CI demands some effort to learn, as you would expect. But, assuming that you already know some PHP, it's quite easy. In fact, the main 'learning curve' I find is that, when you know the standard PHP way of doing something, you tend to do it that way. Only later on, when you are looking in the CI User Guide for something else, do you realize that you could have done the first thing much more quickly and simply with a CI class or helper.

Speaking personally, I found two CI classes quite difficult to understand and follow. These are the XMLRPC class, and the Validation class. This is largely because they both require interface between different pages, or different sites, in order to work, and it is sometimes difficult to get this set up properly. (See Chapters 9 and 8, respectively)

I also found it difficult at first to follow the way CI uses its 'super-object'—see Chapter 7. Getting that right may be the steepest CI learning curve, and mistakes can lead to some odd and frustrating results until you understand it.

The rest: easy. If in any doubt, you can always explore the source code.

Summary

In this chapter, we've looked at some coding examples, bringing together a lot of the functions , which we've discussed bit by bit in the preceding chapters.

We've also looked at the way CI helps:

- To organize your site
- To make coding simpler
- To add functionality

I hope this book has persuaded you that, if you want to code dynamic websites in PHP, CI is a very smart way to do it.

It's also a tribute to the open-source movement, and to the generous people who support it, that such a rich collection of code is available, freely and universally. Thanks, Rick!

Taking this theme of generosity further, the last chapter in this book looks at some other ways you can develop your CI coding—the community of CI users who can (and usually will) provide help, support, and additional code resources.

15
Resources and Extensions

Well, we've looked at CI pretty thoroughly, and I hope you're impressed. We've also developed some of our own code in the process. I'm sure when you looked at some of my code, you started thinking "I could write that better...". Everyone has their own style, and CI allows you a lot of freedom.

The CI Community is full of people who write good code, and luckily many of them are prepared to make it available free of charge to the rest of us. So there's a lot of code out there that may save you a lot of work. If, to take one example, you want to create dynamic graphs of data drawn from your database, you could sit down and write the code yourself, but in fact, at least three people have already tackled this problem, and all of them have made their code available to you.

This last chapter looks at some of the resources you can draw on, to make your coding quicker and easier. CI has a thriving and active community of users and the available resources are changing all the time, so I haven't tried to produce an exhaustive list, just give you an idea of what's there and where to look.

There's a cautionary note too. There is so much code out there that it can easily be confusing. People write their pet projects, some brilliant, some just quite good. Many of us are better at writing code than writing explanations or comments. As a result, it can be quite difficult to work out just what each library or plug-in does, and whether it's the best one for you.

So, let's spend the last chapter of this book looking at the available help.

- Firstly, let's look at the sources of code.
- Then, let's look at a few subjects and compare the code that's available.
- Lastly, let's look at more general sources of help: on PHP, MySQL, and Apache.

CI's User Forums

CI has two main resources:

- The user forums, at `http://www.codeigniter.com/forums/` offer a lively and pretty well continuous discussion of most CI issues. Comments and suggestions made are not always helpful (or accurate), but there are a number of 'senior members' who usually make a lot of sense. It's quite a kind forum, too; people ask very obviously 'newb' questions, but get patient and helpful replies. Occasionally, Rick Ellis himself chips in, but he quite rightly doesn't try to field every issue himself.

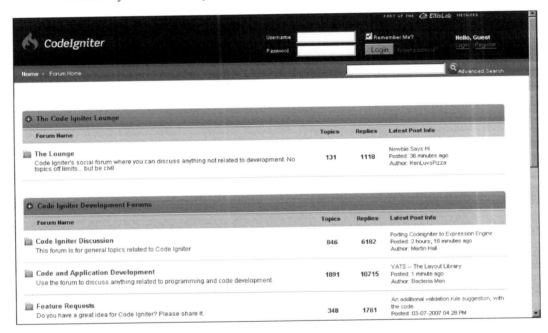

- The wiki, at `http://www.codeigniter.com/wiki/` .This is intended as a "repository for tips, tricks, hacks, plugins, and enhancements." It contains a lot of useful code, although coverage is not systematic.

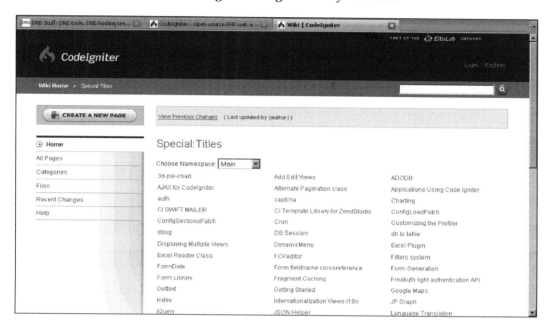

Using the forum or the wiki is easy: you just create a membership for yourself (free) and then log on and do your thing.

If you are seriously using CI, it's worth setting your RSS reader to subscribe to the 'recent changes' feed on the Wiki.

Remember, though, that:

- Not all plug-in writers are as technically competent as Rick Ellis. Their products may have bugs or issues.

- Some of the older plugins written before CI version 1.5 came out may need altering, because the way that libraries were initialized was changed (see Chapter 12). This should not be too difficult to do, but it does mean these library files won't work straight out of the box.

Video Tutorials

If you want to be literally talked through your first CI application, there are three excellent video tutorials on the CI site.

- An introduction to CI.

- Create a blog in 20 minutes. Derek Jones builds basic blog pages, showing you how to set out the site, make database queries, and present the results in views.

- A link to an external video by Derek Allard (see `http://video.derekallard.com/`), which describes, among other things, how to use the Scriptaculous library to integrate AJAX and JavaScript effects. Using the view below, this shows you how to build an auto-complete text entry dropdown, using Ajax to update it.

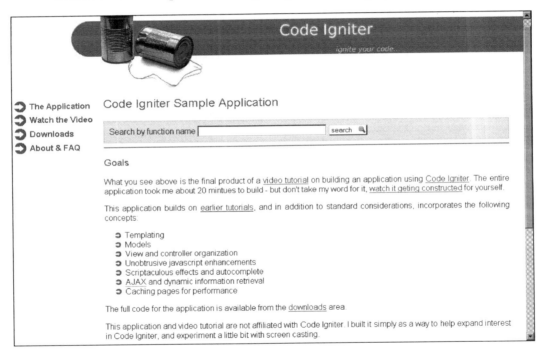

Available Plug-ins and Libraries

Rick Ellis's intention and hope was that CI users would contribute 'plug-ins' or libraries to help other CI users. The framework has only been available for about a year, but already there is a lot of interesting code available.

The number of plug-ins and libraries is growing steadily, and those already there are being changed. So the next section is not a systematic account of what's there: just a few notes on some of the things you might find useful. I'm sorry that I've had to miss out a lot of good stuff: please do look at the wiki yourself.

AJAX/JavaScript

The wiki contains two AJAX packages: one using XAJAX, and the other the prototype.js/scriptaculous.js libraries.

Name	Ajax for CI 1.5.1
URL	`http://www.codeigniter.com/wiki/AJAX_for_CodeIgniter/`
Uses the `prototype.js` and `scriptaculous.js` libraries	
Download includes `.js` files as well as `.php` and a full User Guide. (This is not easy to understand if you don't already have a good grasp of AJAX and the DOM, and it could usefully have had some longer examples.) Simple to install: place the `.php` file in your `application/libraries` folder and the `.js` files in your root directory.	
Newly released, so very few comments on the CI Forums.	
Author	siric

Name	XAJAX
URL	`http://www.codeigniter.com/wiki/XAJAX/`
A CI 'front end' for the XAJAX library. Includes its own JavaScript 'include' file, `xajax.js`	
Author	Greg McLellan—based on the xajax php library (see `http://www.xajaxproject.org/`)

Authentication

Wiki users have also wrestled with security: these three packages look at authenticating your users and avoiding the possible pitfalls of storing session data in cookies.

Name	FreakAuth_light
URL	`http://www.4webby.com/freakauth/`

This includes a library to perform
- user login/logout
- user registration
- remember password
- change password
- website reserved areas locking

a backend administration application to:
- manage users
- manage administrators

It allows you to set four levels of access (from superadmin down to guest) and then to set a 'check' method in controllers. This can be set either in the controller constructor or in individual functions. If a user invokes the controller (or the individual function) the code checks that he/she is logged in, consulting

There's an extensive discussion of this code going on in the CI forums at the time of writing. Some errors have been identified, but the code is now on its third release and it looks as if the problems are being resolved.

Author	danfreak

Name	Auth
URL	`http://www.codeigniter.com/wiki/auth`

This package offers login/logout functionality, registration, with activation, and even a forgotten password reset. It's quite complex to set up: you have to set up a database table, include some new core libraries and helpers, and also do some configs.

Works with CI 1.5.

Author	Anonymous

Name	DB Session

URL	`http://www.codeigniter.com/wiki/DB_Session/`
	`http://dready.jexiste.fr/dotclear/index.`
	`php?2006/09/13/19-reworked-session-handler-for-code-`
	`igniter`

Alters the CI session class (see Chapter 6) which stores session data in cookies. (Which can be encrypted, of course.) This class only stores a session identifiers: you add an extra table to your database, and it looks up all the rest of the session information there.

Works with CI 1.5.

Author	dready

External Sites

There are some 'power users' of CI who contribute code of their own. One good example is Glossopteris, a site run by a US web design company. This makes available some of their own libraries, for instance (at `http://www.glossopteris.com/journal/post/table-relationships-in-ci`) another CRUD library, which they claim "will allow for complex table inter-relationships to be assigned and simple CRUD actions to be completed." This follows the Rails precedent quite closely: you can define relationships between tables such as 'has one' and 'has many' links. The code is available, but could do with more comments or a user guide.

Another development is CI_Forge (`http://www.ciforge.com/`), which is intended as, "A place for projects designed to enhance or extend the lightweight PHP framework CodeIgniter." It provides Subversion and Trac hosting, a wiki, a bug/issue tracker, and change log support. This is a new application, but (as at July 2007) already hosts 20 projects.

Comparisons: Which Charting Library to Use?

That's quite a range of options. Sometimes, there can be almost too much choice.

To demonstrate this, let's look at three options for doing the same thing, and see how they differ. Making dynamic charts of data is not an easy thing to code on your own. But it does make your site look good.

Let's look at three add-ons available for CI that do just this, and try to compare their strengths and weaknesses, as well as look at the results they produce.

Name	3d-pie-chart
URL	`http://codeigniter.com/wiki/3d-pie-chart/`
Generates a pie chart from two arrays of data (labels and values) and saves it on your site. Looks great, but this is all it does. 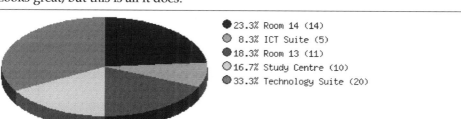 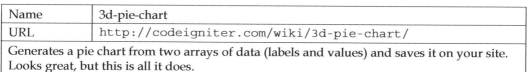	
Simple to set up: put the `piechart.zip` file in your `application/libraries` folder, and write a controller based on the example. Requires a font, and you need to modify a view to display the results. Works with CI version 1.5	
Author	Craig

Name	Panaci
URL	`http://bleakview.orgfree.com/` or `http://codeigniter.com/wiki/Charting/`

Dynamically generates charts and graphs, including bar, line, area, step, and impulse charts (but not pie charts). The wiki entry states: "Please note, this is NOT a commercial grade library such as jpgraph or chartdirector, but it is quite adequate for basic plots". The code example, and specimen plot, below, show what it looks like and how to use it.

```
function graph()
{
  $data_2001 = array(43,163,56,21,0,22,0,5,73,152,123,294);
  $data_2002 = array(134,101,26,46,22,64,0,28,8,0,50,50);
  $Labels = array('Jan','Feb','Mar','Apr','May','Jun','Jul','Aug','Sep','Oct','Nov','Dec');

  $this->chart->setTitle("Annual Rainfall","#000000",2);
  $this->chart->setLegend(SOLID, "#444444", "#ffffff", 2);
  $this->chart->setPlotArea(SOLID,"#444444", '#dddddd');
  $this->chart->setFormat(0,',',',');

  $this->chart->addSeries($data_2001,'dot','2001 ', SOLID,'#00ff00', '#00ff00');
  $this->chart->addSeries($data_2002,'area','2002 ', SOLID,'#ff0000', '#00ffff');

  $this->chart->setXAxis('#000000', SOLID, 1, "2001");
  $this->chart->setYAxis('#000000', SOLID, 2, "Rainfall in MM");
  $this->chart->setLabels($Labels, '#000000', 1, HORIZONTAL);
  $this->chart->setGrid("#bbbbbb", DASHED, "#bbbbbb", DOTTED);
  $this->chart->plot('./images/file.png');

  $this->load->view('graph');
}
```

Will produce the chart below:

Works with CI version 1.5. As with 3d-pie-chart, you copy the file into your `application/ libraries` folder, and call it from your controller, supplying basic parameters and an array of data.

Short discussion in CI Forums, no major bugs found at time of writing.

Author	Oscar Bajner

Name	JP Graph
URL	`http://codeigniter.com/wiki/JP_Graph/`

This is not strictly a plug-in: it's code that allows you to interface between CI and the external JP Graph library. You need to download the JP Graph library, create a series of plug-ins for each graph type you want to use, and then call the plug-ins from a controller as you need them.

As these examples form its website, `http://www.aditus.nu/jpgraph/features.php` show, JP Graph offers a much wider range of charts, and they look great.

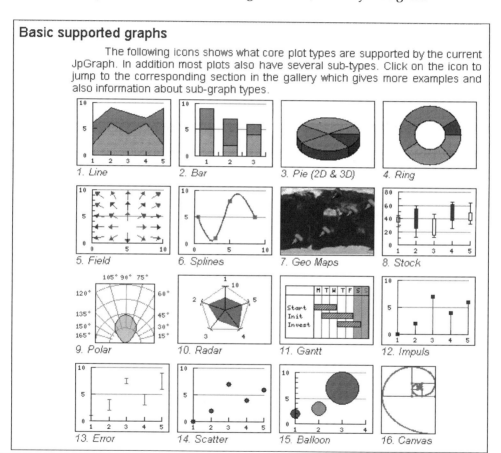

Basic supported graphs

The following icons shows what core plot types are supported by the current JpGraph. In addition most plots also have several sub-types. Click on the icon to jump to the corresponding section in the gallery which gives more examples and also information about sub-graph types.

1. Line
2. Bar
3. Pie (2D & 3D)
4. Ring
5. Field
6. Splines
7. Geo Maps
8. Stock
9. Polar
10. Radar
11. Gantt
12. Impuls
13. Error
14. Scatter
15. Balloon
16. Canvas

There are two disadvantages with JP Graph. As the wiki entry says: "Keep in mind that JpGraph has a very large codebase, so be sure to include only the specific libraries you need for each chart." Secondly, JP Graph is free for personal use, but not for commercial use.

Author	Aditus Consulting

Three options: the first two relatively simple, the second more complex. It depends on what you need (and if you are prepared to pay).

CRUD: the Final Frontier

You need to write CRUD pages in almost every application. It seems simple, and logical, to automate the process of creating those pages! They are tantalizingly standard—and yet they have deceptively large numbers of possible variations. It's impossible to write one without starting to impose your own rules and assumptions on the user. Also, there is always a trade-off between covering more and more possible options on the one hand, and simplicity of use on the other. The more exceptions and possibilities you try to cover, the more complex your code becomes and the larger the download is.

So, quite a few people have had a go at simplifying the basic CRUD operation.

We tried our hand at developing our own CRUD application in Chapter 13. This was a fairly simple model that cut a lot of corners and only allowed you to use a subset of the available HTML form objects; but it does manage to incorporate CI's validation functions.

We've already mentioned, in this chapter, the Glossopteris library.

Another interesting approach is 'CodeCrafter', which is listed on the CI wiki and available from Datacraft Software Consulting in South Africa, at: `http://www.datacraft.co.za/index.php?contents=codecrafter/codecraft`. This claims that, "CodeCrafter will help you generate your entire CodeIgniter application in just seconds." It comes with a 26 page online manual, which shows you how to use its interface to generate CI code. This is a different method to most of the other offerings reviewed here: it builds the CI code for you, using a graphical interface, rather than providing libraries or code for you to patch in.

SuperModel (see `http://codeigniter.com/wiki/SuperModel/`) claims: "The SuperModel Library is an extension to models to automate most of the mundane form-generation and validation tasks. Think of it as scaffolding on steroids."

The author's comments explain the frustrations of writing this sort of code—and also the risk for users. He says: "Please note this library is a work-in-progress. I am currently making many changes, including API changes that will break applications. As I write this (May 30/2006) I am working on implementing one<>many and many<>many joins......It's impossible to write something like this, but stay as flexible like CodeIgniter is. Unfortunately, this library forces you into doing some things a certain way. I've tried to be as flexible as possible, but at the same time, there has to be a line drawn between being flexible, and being completely bloated. That's why this is an external 3rd party library—you're free to implement models the way you want, or use some other similar 3rd party library that does something similar."

Resources for Other Programmes, e.g. Xampplite, MySQL, PHP

There are a lot of useful resources for PHP. Let's just touch on some of them briefly.

- PHP itself can be downloaded free from www.php.net, which also includes a full manual.

- A low-cost PHP editor can be bought from MP Software at http://www.mpsoftware.dk/.

There are many good books on PHP, including *PHP Programming with PEAR*, by Carsten Lucke, Aaron Wormus, Stoyan Stefanov and Stephan Schmidt, published by Packt.

To run a local web server on your own machine, try looking at http://www.apachefriends.org/en/index.html—a site that offers free downloads of the XAMPP package. This installs an Apache web server with MySQL, PHP, and Perl. If the XAMPP package is too comprehensive for you, try Minixampp from the same site, on which the code used in this book was written.

MySQL too has its own web page—http://www.mysql.com/—though if you want to download the latest versions for free, go to http://dev.mysql.com/. (Bear in mind though that many ISPs don't use the latest versions. Although MySQL is up to version 5, most ISP's are still using Version 4. This prevents you using some of the more interesting new features, like stored procedures.) See, *Creating your MySQL Database: Practical Design Tips and Techniques*, by Marc Delisle, published by Packt.

Although MySQL comes with its own tools, the most popular (and most common) tool is PHPMyAdmin. (See *Mastering phpMyAdmin 2.8 for Effective MySQL Management*, also by Marc Delisle, published by Packt.)

Summary

In this Chapter, we've looked at some of the resources available to you when you start to code with CI. There's a lot of ready-made code available. You have to look before you use: don't just take the first plug-in or library that seems to do what you want and start using it. You need to study each offering to see what it really does, and it also helps to go through the code and make sure you understand it. However, if you are prepared to do this, you can find libraries at different levels of scope and complexity that will take on many of the tasks that would otherwise have involved a lot of hand coding.

In particular, we looked at libraries for

- AJAX and JavaScript
- Authentication
- Charting
- CRUD

Lastly, we looked at some of the resources available for PHP and MySQL and for running a local web server.

Index

A

Active Record class
about 51-53
advantages 54, 55
automatic functionality 54
queries, creating 59, 60
queries, deleting 61
queries, reading 56, 57
queries, updating 59, 60
query results, displaying 58
time, saving 54
with default query styles 61
array
about 189
parameters 190

B

benchmarking class 121

C

charting libraries
about 235
comparing 235-237
classes, CodeIgniter
add ons 181-183
date helper 141
inflector helper 141
language class 141
text helper 141
code, testing
end-to-end tests 112
need for 111, 112
unit testing 112
uses of CodeIgniter 112

CodeIgniter. *See* **also CodeIgniter site**
about 12
advantages 7-11
config files, using 24
configuration file 24
configuration settings 51
disadvantages 16, 17, 226
downloading 22
file structure 23
file types 23
for communication 127
framework 12
installing 22
interface problems 171
license 18
open source business model 15, 16
prerequisites 21
requirements 22
setting up 21
syntax rules 33
testing 25
URL helper 46
uses 7
version changes 177
CodeIgniter site. *See* **also CodeIgniter**
architectural issues 73
class types 34
designing 85, 86
file types 34-36
navigating 86-90
table structure 37
configuration settings, CodeIgniter
configuration file 51
database 52
dbdriver 52
hostname 52

password 52
username 52
controllers
default controller 33
designing 39-41
parameters, getting to function 40, 41
syntax rules 34
welcome controller 31
copy by reference 103
CRUD
about 185, 238
array 189
concept 186
data, reading 195
defining 189
functions 192
insert 201
insert2 208
parameters 190
showall 192
test suite 209

D

database
designing 53
setting up, for website 63-66
database tables
about 189
rules 189
date helper
about 142
date formats 142
date formats, converting 143
time zones, generating 143, 144
diagnostic tools 174
display model 78, 79
dotest model
about 216
database, reading from 221-223
database, writing to 22-223
parameters, switch statement 221
report 220
table information, generating from database
query 216
test loop 218, 219
test report, printing 223, 224

test types 221
download helper
about 158
database, downloading as a text file
158-160

E

email class
working with 136-139
error handling class 113

F

file helper
about 156
arrays, comparing 157
file, writing 156
loading 156
file upload class
about 160
loading 160
working of 160-165
form helper
about 74
advantages 74-77
forums
CodeIgniter forum 230
CodeIgniter wiki 231
framework
about 12
PHP frameworks 13
Rails 13
Ruby on Rails 13
FTP class
remote files, testing 127-129

I

image class
about 165
crop, fucntions 166
fucntions 166
resize, fucntions 166
resizing 166, 167
rotate, fucntions 166
watermark, fucntions 166

inflector helper **145**
insert **201**
insert2 **208**
interface problems
  about 172
  CodeIgniter version changes 177
  config files 173
  databases 172
  diagnostic tools 174
  OS difference 173
  PHP version difference 173
  URLs 172

L

language class
  about 146
  webpage, translating 146-149
library class
  for security 92

M

menu
  creating 48

N

nested views
  about 70
  header view, creating 70-72
  parameters 72

O

objects
  about 99
  super-object 100
OOP
  about 99
  objects 99

P

PHP syntax
  long syntax 69
  short syntax 69
plugins and libraries
  AJAX package 233

authentication packages 233, 234
  charting libraries 235-237
  CRUD 238
  external sites 235
  JavaScript package 233
profiler class **122**

Q

queries, Active Record
  creating 59, 60
  deleting 61
  reading 56, 57
  results, displaying 58
  updating 59, 60

R

remote files
  testing, FTP class used 127-129
resources
  CodeIgniter forum 230
  CodeIgniter wiki 231
  MySQL 239
  PHP 239
  video tutorials 232
  XAMPPLite 239
Ruby on Rails **13**

S

security/sessions
  library class 91, 92
  sessions, turning into security 94-96
session class **91**
showall **192**
standard controller **187**
super-object
  code, adding 105, 106
  drawbacks 106-108
  log, tracing 101
  working with 100-103

T

table class
  about 150
  HTML tables, writing 150-152

pages, caching 152, 153
text helper
  about 145
  inflector helper 145
  strings, truncating 145

U

unit test class 115
unit testing
  about 112
  controlling 124
  criteria 117, 118
  example 118-120
  mock database, testing with 123
  timing 124

V

validation class
  about 79
  controller, setting up 81
  forms, setting up 81, 82
  validation, setting up 80
version changes, CodeIgniter
  library classes, initializing 179

model, calling 178
model, loading 178
updating 179-181
views
  designing 37, 39
  nested views 70-73
  syntax rules 34
  working with 32
  writing 67-69

X

XMLRPC
  about 129
  debugging 134, 135
  exchanges, formatting 132-134
  issues 135, 136
  server-client communication 131, 132

Z

zip class
  about 169
  file, compressing 169

Learning jQuery

ISBN: 978-1-847192-50-9   Paperback: 380 pages

Better Interaction Design and Web Development with
Simple JavaScript Techniques

1. Create better, cross-platform JavaScript code

2. Detailed solutions to specific
    client-side problems

PHP Web 2.0 Mashup Projects

ISBN: 978-1-847190-88-8   Paperback: 250 pages

Create practical mashups in PHP grabbing and
mixing data from Google Maps, Flickr, Amazon,
YouTube, MSN Search, Yahoo!, Last.fm, and
411Sync.com

1. Expand your website and applications
    using mashups

2. Gain a thorough understanding of
    mashup fundamentals

3. Clear, detailed walk-through of the key PHP
    mashup building technologies

4. Five fully implemented example mashups with
    full code

Please check **www.PacktPub.com** for information on our titles

PHP Programming with PEAR

ISBN: 1-904811-79-5   Paperback: 250 pages

XML, Data, Dates, Web Services, and Web APIs

1. Maximize your productivity through the use of proven, powerful, reusable PHP components

2. In-depth coverage of a range of important PEAR packages

3. Many code examples provide a clear and practical guidance

AJAX and PHP: Building Responsive Web Applications

ISBN: 1-904811-82-5   Paperback: 275 pages

Enhance the user experience of your PHP website using AJAX with this practical tutorial featuring detailed case studies

1. Build a solid foundation for your next generation of web applications

2. Use better JavaScript code to enable powerful web features

3. Leverage the power of PHP and MySQL to create powerful back-end functionality and make it work in harmony with the smart AJAX client

Please check **www.PacktPub.com** for information on our titles